DREAMLADY.COM

Guidance From Your Dreams

By Marilyn Peterson and Thomas W. Sonandres

SPICA BOOKS
Sun City, Arizona

Grateful acknowledgement for permission to use the cover photo
of the constellation Virgo and its first-magnitude blue-white star Spica,
located near the bottom of the back cover, is made to
Till Credner, Allthe Sky.com.

Copyright © 2003 by Marilyn Peterson and Thomas W. Sonandres

Published by Spica Books, 9742 N. 105th Dr., Sun City, AZ 85351

All rights reserved, including the right of
reproduction in whole or in part in any form, except
for the quotation of brief passages in a review, without
prior permission in writing from the authors,
who may be contacted at www.dreamlady.com.

ISBN 0-9728531-0-3

Design by Thomas W. Sonandres

Printed in the United States of America

First printing February 2003
First edition

DreamLady says that our dreams are not trying to frighten or conceal, but:

- Get our attention
- Preview important happenings
- Assist us mentally, emotionally, financially, physically
- Help us to build a happy, prosperous, and fulfilled life

According to DreamLady, dreams have:

- Led sales people to prospects
- Warned parents of potential health concerns about their children
- Told graduate students of oral exam questions
- Identified root causes of disturbing emotions
- Answered lifetime questions

From www.dreamlady.com, a web site pioneering online dream analysis, DreamLady has responded to more than 10,000 dreams:

- At no charge
- At length
- Individually, not with automated lists of key symbols
- To all dreams, not a few "winning" submissions

Now, *DreamLady.com,* the book, provides the means for you to realize what innately you already are -- the best interpreter of your own dreams. It offers:

- Numerous practical suggestions for your own dreams
- Step-by-step, easy-to-read guidance
- One hundred real dreams that have helped real people

Visit www.dreamlady.com for more information about dreams, memberships, and free interpretations.

To Janis, who gave me my first dream journal.
Tom

DREAM 001

I was hitchhiking with Fred in a city. It was daytime. Lots of traffic. We somehow became separated as I came to a traffic light at a big intersection. I paused, wondering what to do, and then I crossed the street and lost him.

I didn't know my destination and was scared. I met a foreign woman, a Norwegian who was sitting on the edge of the road. I first saw her in the distance off to my left, but sitting on the right side of the road. I walked just past her, stopped, and turned. She was on my right. The woman was wearing a long, dark parka with her hair tucked in underneath and a hood over her head. I asked how to get to New London. She didn't know, but invited me to walk with her. She was big-boned, stoic, calm, and self-confident. Because of her serenity and confidence, I decided to walk with her. I was comfortable. I may have been on a train here, but I don't remember. We wound up at the house of some people, also from Norway. It wasn't clear if they were her friends or if they had rapidly become her friends, but her rapport with them was strong. I didn't stay long. I sensed I didn't belong and, in any event, I'm not a party person.

I departed and was walking again, feeling peaceful. I was on a dirt road covered with snow. It was nighttime. A breathtaking scene of white snow and illuminated darkness surrounded me. It wasn't cold at all. I wore something lightweight. Someone tall was with me, but I was unclear at first if it was Fred or Charles. Fred is short, so it must have been Charles. I was happy. Then, straight ahead, I saw the most beautiful thing I have ever seen: a huge double moon over the snow in the night sky. One moon was on the right horizon and the other on the left. They were slowly moving toward each other, climbing toward the zenith.

I spoke excitedly to Charles, who was standing on my left. "Look, a double moon!" I went fumbling for my camera, but when I got it out, the moons were starting to fade. I was really trying to get the camera functioning, but my film was all screwed up and it wouldn't work. The camera jammed. The moons completely faded out. They had come very close to each other overhead, but disappeared before touching. At the same time, the tall man faded away. I felt some disappointment, but this instantly dissolved because of the next scene.

I was walking slightly ahead on the same road and saw off to the right a big snow bank and, beyond, a field of snow. There I saw Rima and Cindy, my yellow labs. It seemed significant that they were on my right, but I didn't know why. It was still a beautifully illuminated night. In the dream, I knew that they had recently died, but there they were. I was so happy. I was with Fred again, on the road, both of us happy and laughing because the "girls" were back with us. It was like the old days, when Fred and I and the dogs were together, all happy. I said, "Let's give them one more romp in the snow!" I ran straight up to them, racing over a snow bank on the side of the road. Fred was somewhere behind and maybe still on the road. The dogs and I embraced outrageously and played, rolling over and over in the snow.

+ + +

Contents

Dream 001 ("Two Moons") — vii

Introduction — xi

Part One - Basic Dream Understanding and Action — 1

    1 The Five Steps of Dream Interpretation — 3

    2 Beginning Dream Analysis — 12

    3 A Chapter of Dream Interpretations — 20

    4 The Nature of the Dream — 35

    5 The Five Steps Expanded — 39

    6 Recurring Dreams and Dream Things — 53

Part Two - Dream Components — 57

    7 Themes — 59

    8 Settings — 62

    9 Plots — 69

    10 Life-Forms and Related Beings — 75

    11 Moods — 81

    12 Potpourri — 84

Part Three - Special Dreams — 93

13	Nightmares and Other Anxiety Dreams	95
14	Historical Dreams	104
15	Transition Dreams of Birth, Death, Dying, and the Dead	108
16	Psychic Dreams	113

Part Four - Last Resorts and Other More Advanced Techniques   117

17	Some Ways To Remember Your Dreams	119
18	More Advanced Dream Analysis	127
19	Dream Log Maintenance	145

Part Five - Conclusion   149

20	A Few Questions and Answers	151
21	Some Memorable Dreams or Your Final Exam	160
22	Finale	174

Part Six - Advanced Dream Analysis   179

23	One Dozen Dreams by Dreamlady	181

Index   203

INTRODUCTION

Dear Dreamer,

Dreams are the most creative art form going. They scare, entertain, intrigue, and tell us amazing things about ourselves and our worlds. That is, they tell us if we listen. For lack of interest or understanding, think of all the free Technicolor entertainment you've missed—your own personal story nightly in prime time.

Dreams are centuries-old phenomena of worldwide interest and a frequent subject of media attention. For example, the lead article in *The Washington Post* business section of Sunday, October 20, 2002, featured a discussion on how the average person's dreams reflect work and home life and on how to use dreams to solve problems.

In the last seven years, I've interpreted over 10,000 dreams e-mailed to www.dreamlady.com, my Web site, from dreamers around the world. My responses contained insights to enable dreamers to have a happier, more prosperous, and fulfilled life. This I did free of charge, analyzing each dream on its own merits. Dreamers have filled my files with heartfelt thanks, telling me that my dream interpretations are on target and very helpful and asking for a book.

Here it is, *DreamLady.com*. The book offers you another way, on your own, to learn how to understand your dreams and how they can benefit you.

It begins with the basics and ends with how I analyze dreams on www.dreamlady.com. The guidance is simple, specific, easy to understand, and step by step. It has one hundred real dreams to work with, all from real people.

This book is the result of forty years of my dream interpretation and thirty more on the part of co-author and collaborator Tom Sonandres, who attended one of my early workshops.

Let me tell you how the DreamLady workshops, Web site, and this book came about.

In the early 1970s, I did a research study on dreams for the president of a small university in Virginia. The project lasted several years and involved several hundred dreams and their interpretations. The results were eventually published in a two-volume set on dreams and dreaming included with the university's Library Series.

I moved on to another assignment, but I had learned a lot about dreams. I understood what others' dreams were telling them, and I felt certain that I could teach people how to learn from their dreams. Within a year, I had developed my dream course and had begun touring U.S. and Canadian cities, where I was featured on talk shows.

At the end of one three-day seminar in Richmond, Virginia, a participant walked up to me and said, "Let's write a dream book together." I accepted! The offer came from a foreign service officer, then assigned to the U.S. State Department, who had driven down from Washington, D.C., to attend the seminar. He told me that he had been working with his dreams for several years, had been struck by the similarity between my approach and his self-taught one, and had gained a considerable amount of new information at the seminar. That was 1978.

We spent several years collaborating on a dream book, submitting several query letters to publishers. But that interest gave way to other pursuits. Tom was assigned to posts in Eastern Europe and South America, then retired and took up other professions. I was busy building a career as an executive in the nonprofit world.

In the mid 1990s, a pioneer Web site designer created a site that gave me the opportunity to expand into nonprofit consulting. I subsequently launched www.dreamlady.com, the best way, I thought, to pass on what I had learned and to help people understand and use their dreams to their benefit.

To the best of my knowledge, I was the first to interpret dreams on the Internet. It was important for me to do this free of charge. That way, everyone could take advantage of the offer. No one would be turned away because of lack of funds or unwillingness to pay for uncertain interpretations.

In the following years, many dreamers e-mailed www.dreamlady.com and asked if I had a book to buy. They wanted to know more about their dreams. I pulled out the old dream manuscript that Tom and I had put together almost twenty years earlier, looked him up—we had been out of contact for fifteen years—and resumed our collaboration. Interestingly, shortly before my phone call, he had also dug out a copy of the manuscript to work on after an assignment teaching Spanish at Arizona State University had ended. He was and still is also involved in several part-time pro bono commitments, including spearheading a local environmental effort to prevent an ill-sited mining venture from devastating a very special Arizona creek.

Today, the DreamLady Web site has been upgraded, expanded, and redesigned. We now offer a wide array of material to help visitors understand their dreams. This includes methods for uncovering your own personal dream symbols, more dream interpretations, and a membership package, which includes a newsletter, chat room, and threaded discussion with experts. You can also inquire about individual dream consultations and scheduling DreamLady's dream workshop in your local area. Best of all, your dreams continue to be interpreted free of charge. Visit us at www.dreamlady.com.

A word on "Two Moons," a humdinger of a dream that appears, a portion at a time, at the end of most chapters. The dream and our analysis are not typical. "Two Moons" is longer, more involved, more memorable, and better recalled than many. Most dreams do not receive such extensive and detailed treatment for lack of time, energy, and motivation. Nor is treatment to this extent possible without the dreamer's feedback and input, as in this instance. We include it so that readers can see a longer dream taken apart and reassembled. This process reveals numerous messages and provides excellent practice, we think, for looking at your dreams.

Our thanks to Till Credner at www.allthesky.com for permission to use the magnificent photograph for the cover. Our thanks also go to the dreamers who gave us permission to use their creative sleep adventures in these pages. The original text has been edited and proper names changed or omitted.

In closing, let me say that Tom and I hope you will find this book and its easy-to-follow guidance helpful. We want you to quickly discover how your dreams can assist you in a life-long adventure you won't want to miss.

So come. Begin to analyze dreams with us. See how others put their dreams to work. You can too.

Sweet dreams,
Marilyn Peterson and Tom Sonandres

6 February 2003

PART ONE

BASIC DREAM UNDERSTANDING AND ACTION

The Five Steps of Dream Interpretation
Beginning Dream Analysis
A Chapter of Dream Interpretations
The Nature of the Dream – Three Lists
The Five Steps Expanded
Recurring Dreams

1 | THE FIVE STEPS OF DREAM INTERPRETATION

The basic five steps to interpret all dreams. One dream analyzed.

The Five Steps of Dream Interpretation on One Page

STEP ONE – RECORD   Immediately write it down.

STEP TWO – TITLE   Sum it up in a few words.

STEP THREE – ASSOCIATE   What do dream images and other things bring to mind?

STEP FOUR – INTERPRET   What's the dream telling you?

STEP FIVE – ACT   What are you going to do?

Step One - Record

On awakening, don't move. Don't open your eyes. Review the dream on your mind's interior screen, briefly and only once.

Then, eyelids up! Quickly write down whatever you remember. Use the pen you left atop the blank journal page that you opened to last night and placed within reaching distance of bedside before dozing off.

Underline what most got your attention. Which was it? The lion, the chase, the jungle, the fear, the jungle snow underfoot, or whether you would reach awake-time before the lion reached your ankle?

Date it.

Step Two - Title

Give your dream movie a title that captures its meaning for you. Go with what grabbed you the most.

If the chase, maybe call it, "One Step Ahead of the Cat."

If the plot and locale, "Track Meet on Jungle Snow."

If the fear, "Strides of Panic."

If nothing comes, quickly jot down "Lion!" or some other working title and move on. You can always come back later.

Step Three - Associate

Some questions to ask:

- Does a dream symbol remind you of any real-life happening, particularly a recent one?

- Did you awake with something bad "running around" your stomach this morning? Was your stomach "growling" because you "bolted" down last night's "prey," also known as dinner?

- Is anything in this dream similar to a past dream?

- Where in your waking moments do you encounter jungle-like heavy going? In the overgrowth in your neglected backyard? In a relationship?

- What comes to mind when you think of lions? They live in a pride; speaking of which, what is the state of yours these days?

* Does jungle snow conjure up anything out of place or frozen, for example, in your psyche or behavior?

- What was going on in your waking life when you last felt that dream fear?

Step Four - Interpret

Write down a simple story of what the dream is telling you. Review what you have written so far. Come up with a theme. Perhaps you'll see one in the dream, the title, and the associations in Steps One, Two, and Three. Perhaps it will be something very much on your conscious mind. Run the theme through the dream's sentences to develop a story.

If you do not readily find a theme, begin with the dream's first sentence anyway and write down possible meanings for each part of the dream. Tie the parts together, as does an author of a story. Doing this has you in good company. Some fiction writers also begin without knowing the end of their stories. In this process, a theme may emerge.

You can also pause to ask questions or examine specific indicators. For example, in a dream of being chased by a lion, you could do the following:

Look for the literal:

- Consider staying in the bus during <u>all</u> of this

afternoon's African safari.

Then consider the symbolic:

- Are you being chased by courage (the lion), which you lack to confront a business or romantic entanglement (jungle)?

- What unsure or cold footing (snow) are you being driven over? Is there something out of place or frozen in your awake life that calls for action? Something that causes a chill when you "step" on it? Something that has you snowed (overwhelmed, lost) and that covers your world?

- Trying to run away from roaring migraines pursuing you in real life?

Remember that you, the dreamer, are the best interpreter of your dreams. Go with your associations and with what makes sense or possible sense to you. Record an obvious message as well as the faint glimmerings of one.

If nothing occurs no matter how quietly you listen, then guess. Write something! Leave more space than usual in your journal to fill in later. You'll likely have more insights after you've practiced dream interpretation longer, told the dream to another, read more pages of *DreamLady.com*, or simply allowed more time to pass.

Step Five - Act

What are you going to do about this dream? Stop eating heavy meals immediately before bedtime? Meditate on where and when in awake life you felt the dream emotion? Call Leo?

Write down some action plan, even if it's only, "Contemplate!"

Sample Dream

Instructions:

Have a pen at the ready, and, if you prefer not to write on these pages, a sheet of paper. Read the following dream and underline what you consider most important (i.e., Step One) or write the key words on the paper.

Before looking at the answer meaningful to the dreamer on p. 9, interpret it on on p. 8 or your worksheet! Jot down a title (Step Two). Note the associations that the underlined words bring to mind (Step Three). Write down any messages or stories that the associations suggest (Step Four). Propose appropriate follow-up actions (Step Five).

The dreamer is a single female thirty-something.

> DREAM 002 - It's a pleasant, sunshiny day. I'm riding my bike alone, having a good time. I come to an ocean shore with small waves washing onto the sand. I pedal across the beach and, as if land biking and water biking were identical, I continue riding straight into the ocean. I am surprised when bike and I tumble over into the water.

Interpret the dream in the space below or on a separate piece of paper. Then see the interpreted version on the next page.

Step One - Record (Underline what most calls your attention.)

> It's a pleasant, sunshiny day. I'm riding my bike alone, having a good time. I come to an ocean shore with small waves washing onto the sand. I pedal across the beach and, as if land biking and water biking were identical, I continue riding straight into the ocean. I am surprised when bike and I tumble over into the water.

Step Two - Title

Step Three - Associate (Write down what you underlined and possible meanings. Guess!)

Step Four - Interpret (Weave what you've written above into a brief story.)

Step Five - Act (Write a possible action the dreamer might take.)

Interpretation of Sample Dream

<u>Step One - Record</u> (Underline what most called your attention.)

> It's a pleasant, sunshiny day. I'm riding my <u>bike</u> alone, having a good time. I come to an ocean shore with small waves washing onto the sand. I pedal across the beach and, as if land biking and <u>water biking</u> were identical, I continue riding straight into the ocean. I am <u>surprised</u> when bike and I <u>tumble</u> over into the water.

<u>Step Two - Title</u>   "Ocean Biking"

<u>Step Three - Associate</u>

general = I date two men, neither aware of the other

<u>bike</u> = I bike back and forth to work; balance

<u>water biking</u> = not a sensible action

<u>surprised</u> = no real-life association

<u>tumble</u> = loss of balance; here, misjudging the conditions, hence the surprise

<u>Step Four - Interpret</u> (As suggested by another)

The dream points to an imbalance (falling off the bike) in life that you're unaware of or not paying attention to (the surprise). It occurred precisely when you entered deepening emotions (water) inappropriately (on a bike). You're riding atop two romances, which are similar in structure and close but separate (the two bike wheels), the one beau not directly connected to or not knowing the other. You make this bike go, and seemingly are in charge, having a good time with two "big wheels." This starts out as fun, but quickly turns into a short-term balancing act. Your handling (i.e., steering the <u>handle</u>bars) of all this has you pedaling for a tumble, with the threesome ending up all wet. Being surprised in the dream that bikes aren't ocean-going could indicate that you're missing how this may end up. So, <u>wake up before the fall!</u> Dreams in which the dreamer cannot link the dream mood to a real-life one could suggest that this is a dream of a future surprise if steps aren't taken to change course.

<u>Step Five - Act</u>

She soon told both boyfriends the truth and chose to amicably end one relationship. She dreamt no more of ocean biking.

+ + +

The Double Moon Dream and Steps One to Five

The long dream preceding the book's table of contents was and continues to be very meaningful to the dreamer. For her, it's still evolving.

With reference to this chapter, she <u>wrote it down</u> (Step One).

She <u>titled it</u> (Step Two) "Two Moons," naming the dream after the most astonishing of many happenings.

Other key aspects included the various roads, which she <u>associated</u> (Step Three) with her love of hiking and adventuring on dirt ways in the out-of-doors along with very special two-legs and four-legs.

The theme of roads fits into the <u>interpretation</u> (Step Four) as segments of her life journey.

One early <u>action</u> (Step Five) she took was to tell the dream to Charles, who appeared in the dream, and later to Charles and a friend at dinner. This was a week after the dream and a week before a dream message became tragically clear.

+ + +

2 | BEGINNING DREAM ANALYSIS

Introduction to signifiers, dream puns, and interpreting specific dreams.

Signifiers

The first of two terms to learn before plunging into dream interpretation is the

> **sig‑ni‑fi‑er** \'sig-neh-FIE-ur\ n. (1973, coined by DreamLady) 1. A convenient term meaning the dream itself or, more frequently, any part of a dream, such as a color, life form, loud bang, fear, sour taste, action, and adverbs or any other part of speech. *The dream panic that paralyzed his every limb was a key ~.*

Therefore, a signifier—we'll use the term frequently—is <u>anything</u> that our dream senses pick up. If it's visible, loud, fragrant, creepy, soft to the touch, or sensed intuitively, it and its accompanying adjectives are signifiers. Two are the <u>white</u> of the sand and the <u>sand</u> itself. Other more obvious ones are the <u>coolness</u> of a breeze, the <u>smell</u> of sea air, the <u>surprise</u> of falling into the water, and the "<u>shhhh</u>" of waves washing on shore.

Signifiers also include:

- What moves and what doesn't
- North, up, and other directions
- The lion as courage and other such symbols
- The lion as a literal lion and other non-symbols

- How you see the dream, for example, via the eyes of your dream body or via a camera-like lens

<u>Key signifiers</u> are what stand out the most:

- The unusual, the distortion or exaggeration of reality, the razzle-dazzle
- Known people who don't look or act like themselves
- Unknown people who intrigue, attract, repel...
- What's missing, lost, or found
- What disappears or reappears
- The puzzling, mysterious, strange
- The dream's lead, be it animal, vegetable, mineral, nothingness, not of the Earth...
- The opening line or other quote that grabs

Dream Puns or Instant Interpretations

A pun is a play on a word that relates to something similar in meaning or sound to something else. For example, last chapter's sample dream had the dream pun "all wet," which referred to the dreamer's tumble into the water and the possibility that she would end up in the wrong or "all wet" if she continued in her same direction.

Dream puns are common, creative, often witty, and always the provider of an instant interpretation. They are also signifiers. A short list of puns from actual dreams and the meanings to their dreamers

- An ape playing tennis = "Monkeying around"
- A man named Barry = "Bury" a current boyfriend
- Mary Stewart = "Marry" Stewart, the man the dreamer was dating
- Wal-Mart = Something "in store" for you?
- Mr. Harriman = A "harried" man
- Riding a very tall horse in a parade = Get off your high horse!
- Two bees in your hand = "To be" or not "to be"?

Beginning Dream Interpretation

Dream analysis time! Enjoy the many signifiers and the many puns with instant interpretations in the dreams that follow.

We'll practice with actual dreams. All five steps are not in these examples. That's later. But every dream is in keeping with the five steps.

This is an exercise in practicing:

- The process of dream interpretation
- Thinking in dream language
- Expanding your analytical horizons

DANGER!

The meanings that follow belong to others. Interpretations are dependent on the context of the dreamers. These examples provide little context and do not begin to list all possible meanings to the dreamers or all possible meanings in all contexts. That is, (1) dreamers are the best interpreters of their dreams and (2) any low scores on this exercise are totally forgiven in advance.

Instructions:

1. Read the dream.
2. Guess the interpretation. If you wish, pretend that it's your dream.
3. Read the dreamer's answer in the box.

Dream Segments and Interpretations

DREAM 003 - A male dreamed he was firing beams from a laser handgun into a rival going out with the same woman he was dating. The beams had little effect.

INTERPRETATION - *The dream told him that his feelings had become laser-like emotional outbursts and "out of hand." It was high time to cool it and let go of possessiveness and venting frustrations, regardless of his anger, jealousy, anguish, and hurt. It was hers to choose boyfriends. It was his to date her or not, to be evolved or not, and to talk to her or not about his feelings.*

+ + +

DREAM 004 - A woman dreams her house is changing into a hut.

INTERPRETATION - *The dream underlines the self-punishment (the low-class hut) that the dreamer was inflicting on herself (abodes often represent the self) for certain everyday behavior toward her family (the house).*

+ + +

DREAM 005 - A dreamer dreams of mowing a friend's lawn.

INTERPRETATION - *The dream told the dreamer that it was time to trim back the minor irritations (long grass) bothering him from a distance (neighbor's lawn). Inaction had allowed these concerns or eye-sores to grow too long in length and time.*

+ + +

DREAM 006 - A dreamer dreams of a minor auto accident.

INTERPRETATION - *The dream reinforced the dreamer's reluctance to visit a relative, not for fear of an accident, but to avoid an emotional crash guaranteed to occur if he went at this time.*

+ + +

DREAM 007 - In this frightening dream, a friend appears with the face of a bear.

INTERPRETATION - *The dream was an indication that, in the eyes of the dreamer, her friend had been overbearing, acting like a bear, too barefaced (lacking tact), a beast, and otherwise exhibiting the negative characteristics that the dreamer associated with bears.*

+ + +

DREAM 008 - In this dream, the dreamer does not feel the snow under his bare feet nor the cold wind.

INTERPRETATION - *This dream may suggest that the dreamer is unfeeling and probably so numb and chilled out about a particular issue that he finds himself unable to feel anything.*

+ + +

DREAM 009 - A workaholic male dreams that a very long truck is slowly turning onto a highway in front of his car, considerably delaying him.

INTERPRETATION - *The dream told him that long work hours (the truck) interfered with his life journey as well as with his drive and motivation (his car). His workaholic ways were not only slowing him down, but for too long an interval were stopping him cold.*

+ + +

DREAM 010 - A male thirty-something, in a relationship going nowhere, dreamt of a long-forgotten high school girlfriend playing a cardboard violin off-key.

INTERPRETATION - *The dream clearly warned that the same old song was going to play out again, and that this relationship, identical to the high school one, was also disharmonious and not genuine. The dreamer chose not to end it, but as foretold, disharmony soon did.*

+ + +

DREAM 011 - A dreamer, who had been reading about the American Revolution, awoke remembering only someone saying the word "Hessian."

INTERPRETATION - *An encyclopedia confirmed that the name referred to German mercenaries, conscripts hired by England from German princes to fight the American rebeling colonists. The dream pointed to a health problem, which the dreamer had been neglecting because of work demands. Similar to the historical Hessian, he had been selling out his own best interests in the name of duty.*

+ + +

DREAM 012 - An office worker dreamt that he was pulling suit jackets, belonging to his boss as well as clients of their business, from a jumble of clothes on the floor. He was tasked in the dream with hanging his boss's jackets in a closet, but the clothes rack was too high to reach. The dreamer was getting nowhere and becoming frustrated until he spontaneously leaped high and was able to hook a hangar, which was holding a jacket, on the rack. He instantly let go and floated gently back down to the floor. He felt very pleased.

INTERPRETATION - *The dream told him how to bring order to the jumble in his work life. All he had to do was take a leap of faith, expend a burst of creative energy, and quickly complete his assignments, letting go of their burdens and frustrations. In this way, he could enjoy the satisfaction of a job well done. The dream spoke to his unhappiness with having to clean up after his boss, extracting and salvaging the boss's prestige and role (suit jackets) from general office/business disorder. The dream proposed that fancy footwork would quickly complete the dreamer's tasks and have the clothes all hanging nicely with the workplace and his boss tidied up. After the jackets are properly back in the closet, the boss's outfit (the office) would be complete and back*

17

together again. A reserve (extra jackets in the closet) would keep it that way. Most importantly, all this would not only end the dreamer's frustrations, it would free him to concentrate on what else he was paid to do: straighten up the clients' mess. He subsequently used some "fancy footwork," which turned out to his benefit.

+ + +

"Two Moons" and Beginning Dream Analysis

The dream began with the dreamer and Fred, her husband, on the road (in this instance, a paved downtown city street). By hitchhiking, a temporary and ad-hoc method of traveling through life, the two were just getting by. In essence, they were going along for the ride rather than living by self-determination. At the time of the dream, they were on amiable terms, but separated and undergoing a divorce.

Key signifiers merit special attention. In this dream, one was the intersection, a crossroads with choices of directions. In the dream and in life, the dreamer was at a busy point, facing tough choices in relationships, residence, and job. Her deliberations were stop and go and back and forth (the stoplight and the traffic). To proceed with this or return to that? The dreamer, however, was not one to stay put for long, notwithstanding unresolved dilemmas or the unknown ahead. So she crossed the intersection.

In this come-what-may move, she lost Fred. By going ahead alone, their path became her path. Now what lay ahead was for her, not him or them. And what was ahead was a woman from Norway in a dark parka, hood up, sitting on the side of the road waiting for her to walk up.

+ + +

A CHAPTER OF DREAM INTERPRETATIONS

3

Five dreams iin the five-step format.

Dream Interpretations

Instructions:

1. Read each dream (Step One – Record).

2. Pause. Before looking at the book's interpretation of each dream, underline what you think are the key signifiers, then come up with your own title, associations, interpretation, and how you would act. You can pretend that this is your own dream or that you are helping another.

3. Compare your answers with the ones given. See how others arrived at their interpretations.

> WARNING! To repeat, the following dreams may have meanings for their dreamers that are different for you. They may also have additional meanings not given here.

4. The objective is to practice dream-think, convert key signifiers into relevant messages, and better understand your dreams.

Practice - Dream 013

Instructions:

Interpret the dream in the space below or on a separate piece of paper. Then compare it with the version on the next page.

Step One - Record (Underline what you think are the key signifiers or what most stands out.)

A wife dreamed this one.

> DREAM 013 - I had a nightmare of a frightening half-dog, half-cat creature crawling toward me through my bedroom window.

Step Two - Title

Step Three - Associate (Write down what you underlined and possible meanings. Guess!)

Step Four - Interpret (Weave what you've written above into a brief story.)

Step Five - Act (Write a possible action the dreamer might take.)

Interpretation - Dream 013

<u>Step One - Record</u> (Underline key signifiers.)

    I had a nightmare of a <u>frightening</u> <u>half-dog, half-cat creature</u> <u>crawling</u> toward me through my <u>bedroom</u> <u>window</u>.

<u>Step Two - Title</u>

"The Dog-Cat Terror"

<u>Step Three - Associate</u>

<u>frightening</u> (dream mood) = a frightening circumstance!

<u>creature</u> = an antagonistic relationship

<u>crawling</u> = something low, underhanded, creepy, approaching

<u>bedroom</u> = rest, privacy, physical intimacy

<u>window</u> = opening to the outside world

<u>Step Four - Interpret</u> (As suggested by another)

Cats and dogs are traditional enemies. In the dream, these two opposites are as close as they can be. This two-halved, Siamese-twin horror is locked into an internal antagonistic relationship, an extremely disturbing nightmare to the dreamer. This is not something she wants to live with. It's crawling its way into the dreamer's privacy, physical intimacy, private marital life, and her place of peace and rest (bedroom). The thing comes from the outside, suggesting that she sees some troublesome contradiction or distortion invading her life from the external environment. The dream tells of some fundamental or functional disagreement or an internal conflict. She may also feel exposed (the open window).

Step Five - Act

Nightmares are extreme alerts that something is out of control emotionally. It may be beneficial for the dreamer to re-evaluate her relationship, work it out in her journal, discuss the dream and its source with her spouse, and explore with him ways to avoid another nightmare.

+ + +

Practice - Dream 014

Instructions:

Interpret the dream in the space below or on a separate piece of paper. Then compare it with the version on the next page.

Step One - Record (Underline key signifiers.)

The dreamer was a person drifting through life.

> DREAM 014 - I awoke hearing a dream rendition of "Somewhere Over the Rainbow." This was catchy and curious. I recalled no images or anything else.

Step Two - Title

Step Three - Associate (Write down what you underlined and possible meanings. Guess!)

Step Four - Interpret (Weave what you've written above into a brief story.)

Step Five - Act (Write a possible action the dreamer might take.)

Interpretation - Dream 014

<u>Step One - Record</u>

>I awoke hearing a dream rendition of "Somewhere Over the <u>Rainbow</u>." This was catchy and <u>curious</u>. I recalled no images or anything else.

<u>Step Two - Title</u>

"Where's the rainbow?"

<u>Step Three - Associate</u>

<u>rainbow</u> = the pot of gold, fortune, goals

<u>curious</u> (dream mood) = I'm intrigued

<u>Step Four - Interpret</u>

My goals remain distant, heard but unseen.

<u>Step Five - Act</u>

Select one goal, list steps to achieve it, take the first step today. Tape the following to the wall:

>Whatever you can do, or dream you can, begin it. Boldness has genius, power, and magic in it. – Goethe

+ + +

Practice - Dream 015

<u>Instructions</u>:

Interpret the dream in the space below or on a separate sheet of paper. Then compare it with the version on the next page.

<u>Step One - Record</u> (Underline key signifiers.)

> DREAM 015 - Night. The sky is star-filled, breathtaking. On a beach, I see two geysers, one more voluminous and higher than the other. I am enthralled with Nature's beauty.

<u>Step Two - Title</u>

<u>Step Three- Associate</u> (Write down what you underlined and possible meanings. Guess!)

<u>Step Four - Interpret</u> (Weave what you've written above into a brief story.)

<u>Step Five - Act</u> (Write a possible action the dreamer might take.)

Interpretation - Dream 015

Step One - Record

> Night. The sky is star-filled, <u>breathtaking</u>. On a <u>beach</u>, I see <u>two geysers</u>, one more voluminous and higher than the other. I am <u>enthralled</u> with Nature's beauty.

Step Two - Title

"The Together Geysers"

Step Three - Associate

general = I'm dispirited of late that a friend is more advanced than I am in metaphysical pursuits.

<u>two geysers</u> = my friend and I; also, channeled but unleashed spiritual (water) energies

<u>beach</u> = the edge of the vast unconscious mind (ocean)

<u>breathtaking</u>, <u>enthralled</u> (dream mood) = awe of the power of the mind and of Nature

Step Four - Interpret

What counts is the spiritual sharing (side-by-side geysers), not different intensities.

Step Five - Act

No comparisons! Be the flow, upward, together, and in joy with this remarkable sister human being. Tell her the dream.

+ + +

Practice - Dream 016

<u>Instructions:</u>

Interpret the dream in the space below or on a separate piece of paper. Then compare it with the version on the next page.

<u>Step One - Record</u> (Underline key signifiers.)

> DREAM 016 - My dentist, standing, is explaining the importance of dental care to attentive patients seated around him. All are inside a circle painted on the floor. I am off to one side, listening engrossed but troubled that I haven't joined the group.

<u>Step Two - Title</u>

<u>Step Three - Associate</u> (Write down what you underlined and possible meanings. Guess!)

<u>Step Four - Interpret</u> (Weave what you've written above into a brief story.)

<u>Step Five - Act</u> (Write a possible action the dreamer might take.)

Interpretation - Dream 016

Step One - Record

<u>My dentist</u>, standing, is explaining the importance of dental care to attentive patients seated around him. All are <u>inside a circle</u> painted on the floor. I am <u>off to one side</u>, listening engrossed but <u>troubled</u> that I haven't joined the group.

Step Two - Title

"Dental Distancing"

Step Three - Associate

general = My dentist filled a cavity three days ago. He said to call if it hurts. It does, but I haven't called.

<u>my dentist</u> = a good professional

<u>inside a circle</u> = encircled by the dentist's care

<u>off to one side</u> = outside his influence

<u>troubled</u> (dream mood) = troubled

Step Four - Interpret

By not phoning my dentist, I am outside his circle of influence.

Step Five - Act

Call him or do not call him, but stop complaining!

+++

Practice - Dream 017

<u>Instructions</u>:

Interpret the dream in the space below or on a separate sheet of paper. Then compare it with the version on the next page.

<u>Step One - Record</u> (Underline key signifiers.)

A woman planning a new business had the following dream:

> DREAM 017 - I am carrying a simple corrugated cardboard box, about one-foot square, into which I have put loose grapes (stripped from their stems). I am walking among a group of people, asking if anyone would like to buy some grapes. To some people I simply ask, "Would you like some?" Only a few people decide to sample any. They are red grapes.

<u>Step Two - Title</u>

<u>Step Three - Associate</u> (Write down what you underlined and possible meanings. Guess!)

<u>Step Four - Interpret</u> (Weave what you've written above into a brief story.)

<u>Step Five - Act</u> (Write a possible action the dreamer might take.)

Interpretation - Dream 017

Step One - Record (Underline key signifiers.)

> I am carrying a <u>simple corrugated cardboard box</u>, about <u>one-foot square</u>, into which I have put <u>loose grapes</u> (stripped from their stems). I am walking among a group of people, asking if anyone would like to buy some grapes. To some people I simply ask, "<u>Would you like some?</u>" Only a <u>few people</u> decide to sample any. They are <u>red grapes</u>.

Step Two - Title

"Loose Grapes for Sale"

Step Three - Associate

<u>simple corrugated cardboard box</u> = a not very elegant container

<u>one-foot square</u> = a small capacity to sell from

<u>loose grapes</u> = unfinished (loose ends), disconnected, lacking ethics

"<u>Would you like some?</u>" = low-keyed sales pitch

<u>a few people</u> = little success

<u>red</u> grapes = energy, power

Step Four - Interpret (As suggested by another)

The dream speaks to limitation. The produce for sale is boxed in a cheap-looking container. Sales are further limited by the small box, grapes sold individually rather than in bunches, and by the sales pitch, "Want some?," which could mean you're giving them away. The dream suggests you're selling yourself short. Your approach is small grapes and not selling. Your energy (red) is scattered and loose. You're selling out if not giving yourself away.

Step Five - Act

If selling "on the street" isn't working, consider going after a more selective group of customers, in larger quantity, with wares more attractively displayed. The dream reinforced the dreamer's efforts to launch a new business, which involved researching manufacturing techniques, goals, and market niche and becoming more visible.

+ + +

"Two Moons" and a Chapter of Dream Interpretations

Root characters are the stuff movies and dreams are made of: heroines and villains, masters and students, and much else. The wise woman is one. She is a universal dream figure of many disguises, but in dream interpretation, universal symbols are best viewed in the context of the dream and the dreamer. In "Two Moons," the Norwegian, who indeed was wisdom incarnate, represented aspects of the dreamer's own higher self, future self, and deep feminine energies. The Norwegian's example suggested that assistance comes from the dreamer's feminine, intuitive nature and from others with direct links to it. The woman of the North taught, again by personal example, how to shift energies from fear to peace and how to rise above life's agitations over external impermanence. This is done by identifying with the feminine energies through a deep tranquility, trust, and knowing; being stoic; and intuitively understanding what is impermanent and permanent.

How wise is someone who cannot tell the dreamer how to get to New London? In this case, extremely wise. The Norwegian, in essence, told her how: namely, that the way to New London was through integration with her deep feminine nature. The Norwegian also knew that to actually get to New London was up to the dreamer. More on New London later.

Key signifiers deserve extra attention. What are other possible meanings of the Norwegian? The dreamer has no conscious ties of blood, friendship, reading interests, etc. to Scandinavia. But she does identify with "north," a word that shares linguistic roots with "Norwegian" and "Norseman," among others. She loves snow and winter, the least active of the four seasons. In winter, growth in Nature is slowest or stops. It's the season most conducive for humans to slow down, meditate, find calm, develop knowing, and, particularly in olden days, sleep and dream more. In "Two Moons," only after her exposure to the woman of the North did the dreamer connect with her deeper self and soon thereafter found herself in a magical snow land of celestial and surface wonders. These are clues to the essential message of the dream.

+ + +

4 | THE NATURE OF THE DREAM

An interlude from dream interpretation to look at the nature of the dream

What Are Dreams?

Adventures
Another reality
Answers
Associations
Consequences
Energy outlets
Lessons
Mysteries
Our messages to ourselves
Practice (rehearsals, tests)
Reviews
Re-balancing
Thought forms, energy forms, mind projections
Time collapsed (simultaneous time or timelessness; past, present, and future are not necessarily separated)
The dreamer
The fourth dimension
The future (alerts, options, rehearsals, tomorrow's script, warnings)
The most creative art form going
The six senses collectively, the meeting of inner and outer senses
Truth

Unfinished business (leftovers, residues, unresolved
   conflicts)
Your real dream journal
Your own personal story in prime time

What To Do With a Dream?

If breathtaking, paint it.
If complex, disarm it.
If entertaining, enjoy it, but also think about the message.
If informative, try it on for size.
If it makes sense (e.g., not harmful), act on it.
If meaningful, study it.
If meaningless, look again.
If memorable, take it to lunch.
If moving, put it to poetry.
If musical, hum it now and again.
If mysterious, play detective.
If persistent, listen before tap-tap becomes clobber-clobber.
If recurrent, take more heed.
If sad or depressing, look for the opportunity, the way out.
If scary, add a happy ending, then find, confront, and
   neutralize the scary source.
If symbolic, hang it on the wall.
If unacceptable, at least respect it.
If unfinished, finish it.

What Can a Dream Do For You?

Advise, alert, answer, inform, point out, remind, reveal, warn
Balance
Challenge
Change, adjust
Depress
Entertain
Encourage, inspire

Frighten
Heal
Help
Integrate
Provide experience
Predict
Puzzle, intrigue
Relieve, vent
Resolve
Sadden
Shake
Sort
Suggest
Support
Teach
Validate

"Two Moons" and the Nature of the Dream

"Two Moons" had almost everything under "What Are Dreams?": adventures, mysteries, the future, and unfinished business with Fred. Another reality took place with the return of the deceased dogs, the instant fade-outs, the second moon in the Earth's sky, and the antiphysics motion of the two moons. This dream is also an excellent example of two other items on this chapter's lists: dreams are the most creative art form going and dreams are your own story in prime time every night.

"Two Moons" had other elements common in dreaming. It was essentially visual and emotional. Images carried the action. Spoken words were significant, but few. The dream was symbolic, not literal. The dreamer was not consciously aware she was dreaming, a state of mind conducive to the suspension of disbelief, to the removal of social restrictions and personal inhibitions, and, once awake, to seeing what we do in the sleep-state with these dream-based freedoms. It also demonstrated another dream truth: The purpose of dreams, essentially, is to help the dreamer.

+ + +

5 | THE FIVE STEPS EXPANDED

An extended explanation of the basic five steps of dream interpretation

The Five Basic Steps of Dream Interpretation Expanded

We expand the basic five steps of dream interpretation to provide you with more ways to understand your dream messages and then benefit from them.

Step One - Record

Start a dream journal if you haven't yet. It can be a commercial dream journal, a three-ring notebook, a spiral notebook with your artwork on the cover, or something else <u>that won't easily come apart</u>. Loose papers too easily become floaters, passing forever out of your life.

Immediately before falling asleep, do the following:

- Have the journal at your bedside within easy reach.

- Each night, open it to the next blank page and place a pen or pencil at the ready.

Immediately after sleep, make three quick moves:

- <u>On awakening, with eyes closed, instantly review the dream.</u> Don't stir. Don't open your eyes. A sudden move and POOF!, the dream or much of it could disappear. Do a quick dream review, from end to beginning, if you like. Look for images, sounds, and feelings. If none, remember your first thought of the day.

- <u>Open your eyes and start writing **without** delay.</u> If you recall several dreams, immediately put to paper at least one word about each so that after writing down the first dream, you'll at least have a word to trigger your memory about a second or third dream. By recording quickly, less of the dream is lost. Memory of a dream can disappear unbelievably fast. The act of awakening often slams shut the trapdoor to your subconscious.

- <u>Record spontaneously.</u> Pour your dream recollections onto the journal pages without concern for complete sentences, spelling, capitalization, and proper sequence. As you're scribbling furiously, if you remember something that happened earlier in the dream, write it down instantly, beginning the sentence with, "Earlier." This way, you put to paper a maximum amount of material without interruption and do so *rápido*.

Some more tips.

Write what you witnessed. Ideally, this pouring forth will have you touching on the following:

- What or who puzzled, intrigued, was missing, was out of place, and changed during the dream. Throw in some adjectives.

- The basics: the setting, time, plot, main characters, and particularly the dream moods during and <u>after</u> the dream. Your awe or terror may reveal the spiritual or slippery nature of your dream snake. Your good feeling or suspicion may help decide whether to take the dream stranger's advice. Your dream flash of anger may link to an awake-life flash, identical or less exaggerated, and to accompanying circumstances, all good clues to the dream's message.

Write down **something**

Jot down in the journal dream segments (for example, an image, a single word, a color, a melody, or your mood on awakening). Dream fragments can be quite meaningful. For example, they may preview, returning in fuller fashion in a future dream. What repeats in your dreams is significant. If you retrieve nothing from your sleep time, put your first thought of the day in your dream journal. That thought could have been at play in your subconscious during the night. By writing it down, you are reinforcing the habit of recording your dreams and wanting to remember them.

Leave space after Step One

Such things as a passing thought, a glance in the mirror, or a colleague's word can trigger more of the dream, moments or hours later.

Here's a checklist for your morning's journal entry. Come back to it later for guidance or to run powerful dreams through it.

The Fill-in-the-Gaps Dream Analysis Checklist

Who?	Who were the main characters? What was your role? Active or passive? What was exaggerated or otherwise different about you or another? Who stood out? Do you know her, him, or them? Strangers are often significant.
What? (plot)	What was the story line? What happened last? What solution was there? What structure appeared? Because-Therefore (i.e., cause-effect)? Beginning-Middle-End?

(time) Any time warps? A quick change of scene? A slow-motion episode? A no-motion paralysis? Also see "Where?"

(props) What props (objects) called your attention?

What words did you recall? They may be significant, particularly if spoken or written in special fashion or vividly remembered.

(puns) Look for plays on words.

DREAM 018 - A dreamer named Marilyn dreamt of a college quarterback calling a power play for the University of Maryland.

INTERPRETATION - *The dream suggested that the Cosmos is summoning something powerful and special for her, particularly because her name is pronounced the same way as the name of the football team.*

(colors) Was there an unusually bright yellow or riveting pale violet? Does a memorable color highlight a significant dream object or other signifier?

(mood) The principal dominant emotion is a <u>critical</u> dream element or signifier, and often is the best link to the source of your dream. Under what awake circumstances did your dream indifference, intensity, fear, or joy appear exactly or in less exaggerated form?

Where? Rome, the moon, underwater? Hilly, noisy, bad smelling, foggy? Look for messages in the descriptions of the locale, the terrain, or other scenery and backdrop.

When?   At night? The past? Spring? Record any clock time or calendar date.

How?   If significant, include these in your analysis.
How much?

Should I write down a lot?

Yes, because recording as many specific things as you can recall provides more data for interpretation. Everything is a clue.

No, if you only have so much recording time before family, work, the airport shuttle, etc., but at least get down what stood out.

Write right brain

Your dream was intuitive, spontaneous, and no-think. This is pure right brain, so right-brain your journal entry. Let the words flow. Capture your dream experience, the mood, and the essence. You are NOT writing for your high school English teacher. No credit for crossing Ts, capitalizing, or writing in complete sentences. This is not the time for conciseness, simplicity, or embellishment. So if what you have written does not proceed logically, is laced with misspellings and run-on sentences, has doodles and other scribbling in the margins, and would otherwise flunk Composition 101, you've got it! The right brain in all its glory. The left brain's impeccable reasoning, polished prose, and checklists can flourish in the rest of the steps. Legibility, however, is important if you want to read later what you wrote.

Go back and underline what was important

Underline (or highlight with a marker) the vivid dream aspects, what you found peculiar, puzzling, frightening, and inspiring, especially anything about your dream self. Underline your dream mood twice.

Add the date and...

...if so inclined, number the dream, categorize it as a nap dream, dream fragment, recurring dream, or other dream type.

> TIP: Soon you'll be writing down all types of dreams and pieces of dreams. This enables you to work with your dreams <u>in a series</u>, which gives you more understanding about the issues in your life and their status. You'll be surprised how much you learn about yourself.

Step Two - Title

Movies have titles. Dreams are movies. So title your dreams. Caption each of your dream-movies with a well-chosen word or more that connects you to it. Titles make your dreams easier to talk about, to separate from other dreams, and to remember the dream contents a day or year after. Besides the titling process, coming up with something descriptive, helps launch the interpretation process.

> DREAM 019 - I dream that I am a soldier in the midst of battle. Troops fight and die. Bombs explode. Bullets whiz by. Someone nearby keeps yelling "attack," but I want to retreat and think that everyone on my side should fall back with me.

Possible Titles	Comment
"Being Against the Order to Attack in the Midst of an Awful Battle"	Very long!
"War's Internal Conflicts, Confusions, Choices"	Long, but better!
"Retreat!"	Good length!

Step Three - Associate

Associate dream signifiers with the other parts of your life, awake or asleep.

Begin with what you underlined in Step One (for instance, the dream mood). How were you and others feeling? Can you trace your dream joy or nostalgia to a similar or a less exaggerated real-life experience? Yours or another's? Yesterday or the day before? Does your dream mood link to any recent indifference or intensity? If you make a connection between dream anger and yesterday-at-5 p.m. traffic anger, you're on to something. Then look for additional links between the dream and circumstances surrounding the 5 p.m. incident.

What associations come with the setting, plot, theme, and main characters? Left-brain the setting with questions. Right-brain it with stillness to see what pops into consciousness.

In each instance of associating the mood, theme, a plot play-action, or other dream aspect, what first comes to mind? What meaning does it have for you?

What likes or dislikes? What may have triggered it?

What do you associate with your dream's pulsating dark forest green? Growth? Nature? Your favorite color? The paint job on a friend's new 4x4? A green in a movie seen last week? If the color is that of a dream bouncing ball, where does that dark green take your memory? Back to some ball bouncing of a younger you, possibly a much-younger you? To a playground? A reminder that growth and play can be one? That life's ups and downs can be handled by seeing them as no big deal, as did the dream kid?

If you have absolutely no clue what the dark-green ball means, pretend the answer will win you $1,000 on a quiz show. Guess something and go on to the next underlining.

Critical in this process of making associations is the real-life context of the dreamer at the time of the dream. What was going on? What thoughts, feelings, and actions impacted on you?

Whichever linkages seem right or possibly right to you are valid interpretations to record and consider.

Possible Triggers of Your Dream Signifiers

Something recent or very much on your mind

A sore back, too-tight pajamas, a pregnancy, a street noise that awakened you, tonight's pig-out, yesterday's heated argument, tomorrow's exam, a decision to rent or buy an apartment or other unresolved dilemma, your last thought before falling asleep, or your first one on awakening.

Something recent but dismissed

Unfinished business, more often from the recent past, or other leftovers. Someone or something seen yesterday, but not focussed on, a friend's comment two days ago that seemed insignificant at the time, last night's unresolved dream, a family problem, a forgotten noise in your house that a distraction kept you from investigating.

Something memorable

A birthday, an anniversary, a dream one year ago, a memory that may or may not have recently flashed through your conscious mind.

Something firmly thought or felt

A belief, goal, ideal, motivation, prejudice, principle, virtue, attribute, joy, fear, or something else very much on your mind.

Something from another reality

A telepathic dream, a fantasy dream, a message from beyond? A future possibility? An inspirational or spiritual guidance dream?

Step Four - Interpet

The objective in this step is to write down what the dream is telling you by connecting clues and weaving them into a story.

Review what you have written so far—the words underlined in Step One, the title of Step Two and the associations of Step Three.

Recall three solid tips:

<u>Look for the literal, then the symbolic.</u>

Did you dream of a flood coming from under the kitchen sink? First, check out the literal. Poke around under it. Nothing loose, wet, corroded? With the literal ruled out, what symbolically is gushing? What in or of the kitchen is causing a flood of emotions (water)? What feelings are not draining properly out of your innards? Or is there something in your internal physical plumbing not going down or coming out right?

<u>Look for dream puns.</u>

The instant interpretation, remember? Lots of puns in the last paragraph and in the next one. Lots of literal and symbolic possibilities to look for in each dream too.

> DREAM 020 - I dreamed of a sad-faced bird.
>
> INTERPRETATION - *Relevant puns may include a call for light-heartedness, some upbeat soaring, or gratitude that even a sad-faced bird in the hand is worth two in the bush. A symbolic meaning, given that birds can be messengers, is that the bird is sad because it knows an unhappy message is en route to your address. A literal interpretation is that it's time to take your canary to the* vet, *clean the cage, or show it more attention.*

<u>Trust your dreams and your interpretations</u>

A dream is interpreted when a meaning feels right, makes sense to you, and has you saying aloud, "That's what it means!"

Four other good interpreting tips:

47

Find a Theme

Look at what you've written, underlined, and titled. Do you see something about a theme? For instance, about health, a relationship, the nature of the problem in a problem-solution dream, or particularly about something related to issues in your daily life? Take a theme through the dream's sentences, developing a vignette or a short story as you go.

If more than one theme comes to mind—dreams have multiple levels of meanings—do a mini-story for each.

Ask questions

Look for dream messages in the answers. See p. 47 for questions in the "flood" dream and answers in the "bird" dream.

Mind anything that repeats

Look for recurring themes and other "repeats" in the dream. Recognizing repetition is a very important key to dream interpretation.

> DREAM 021 - A woman was ill at ease in a dream with a female and, later, a male. The next night, she dreamt that she was entirely comfortable removing mold in a restaurant sink.
>
> INTERPRETATION - *The recurring theme was about the dreamer's comfort level. The second dream suggested that she might best go to work at a restaurant or other menial job, do a better clean up after eating, or get rid of unhealthy growths due to neglect and inactivity. This dream pointed to one or more of these areas to direct her masculine and feminine energies to and away from spending time in uncomfortable female and male relationships of no consequence. The dream encouraged her to pursue new employment opportunities.*
>
> +++

Practice

Continue to record and interpret your dreams in your journal. Tell others your dreams and ask for feedback. Read on for advanced dream interpretation, with more about dream meanings and, more importantly, about the interpreting process. See how others, in their life's context, interpreted dream signifiers similar to those in your dreams. Take actions on your dream messages that make sense and are beneficial, a practice that encourages new dreams.

Step Five - Act

Dreams call for implementation. Do something beneficial and not harmful. Ignoring dream themes and messages may not make them go away.

Action may only be to contemplate or to sort dream issues out to the extent possible in your own mind, then let them go. Or you can study the dream, take note, and pat yourself on the back. Sometimes just thinking about our choices, for example, is enough to move future dreams to a point at which they offer us more helpful details.

Action may also entail more outgoing responses, such as telling the dream to another, curbing your wordiness, addressing a family problem, or going to see a doctor.

> DREAM 022 - In a recurring dream, the dreamer is violently engulfed by a tidal wave.
>
> INTERPRETATION - *The dream suggests that a powerful emotional force (the wave) is overwhelming her, again and again (recurring dream). However, the dreamer, a centered and peaceful individual, could not identify the real-life source of the wave.*
>
> ACTION: *The dreamer told the dream to a friend, who suggested that she look harder at the meaning of this wall of engulfing water. Tidal waves or tsunamis can be triggered by distant (offshore) disturbances (quakes).*

She was asked if the tsunami could be the emotional (water) outbursts (tidal waves) created at a distance from the dreamer but directly threatening her tranquility. This series of dreams pointed out to her that a certain family member's quick temper, displaying itself outside the home (offshore) and occurring over and over again, had become more disturbing to her than she had realized.

+ + +

DREAM 023 - A young man awoke from the dream of a favorite uncle preparing tasty, well-fried hamburgers. He also awoke with a stomachache.

INTERPRETATION - *The man quickly concluded, thanks to the dream, that a noon meal of half-cooked, wolfed-down hamburgers, prepared by a friend, was the cause of his stomachache. His dream had contrasted the correct way to cook a burger with the incorrect way the dreamer experienced in real life.*

ACTION: *He took much more care with what he ate, even if the chef was a friend.*

+ + +

A Short List of Some Actions Said to Resolve Any Problem

- Do
- Delegate
- Delay
- Drop

A Longer List

- Acquire unconditional love
- Be of good cheer
- Call Claude, about whom you dreamed

- Contemplate
- Count your blessings
- Eat more carrots
- Forgive
- Identify the problem
- Take baby steps toward a solution
- Take control
- Take total responsibility
- Tell the dream to another
- Test this or that

It is said that there are at least ten solutions to every problem. So choose the best remedy and then take one constructive <u>step</u>.

"Two Moons" and the Five Steps Revisited

Asking questions and looking for recurring signifiers are two very important keys to understanding dreams.

Why did the dream give so much attention to the camera, a seemingly nondescript prop?

The camera was significant. It triggered the disintegration of the scene with the twin moons. At the moment the dreamer wanted a picture of this extraordinary celestial occurrence, the camera acted up, Charles disappeared, the two moons faded away, and the dreamer suddenly found herself alone on the road for the third time in the dream.

But what was the meaning of the jammed camera and, before that, of the fumbled camera and screwed-up film?

Cameras capture impermanence, freeze-framing a moment never to return. The focus of the dream was not on the non-merging of the two moons, but on the merging of the dreamer and her two female dogs. At this point, she needed no camera to capture the permanence of bonds and incredible joys that never die. Besides, a photograph of the two moons might have given her a clear picture or a record, in advance, of the fatal significance of the fading out of Charles. With the rarest of exceptions, dreams do not tell us of literal deaths.

+ + +

6 | RECURRING DREAMS AND DREAM THINGS

> What recurs in your dream life is what isn't being addressed.

Recurring Dreams and Dream Things...

...reveal important ongoing issues calling for our attention. What repeats may be the same dream or close variations, and more frequently, the same dream signifier—a theme, location, plot, character type, etc.—in separate dreams or the same dream. Their sources may include such things as an unfinished goal, a stuffed hurt, a perceived lack, or an unattended fear. They pop up repeatedly because the dreamer is not acting on them in real life.

What repeats in dreams is usually more significant than what doesn't. Recurring dreams and dream signifiers over a short time span (a few days, for example) are repeat signals from the subconscious that something now needs to be addressed. Occasional repeats over the months and years deal with life themes and other longer-range matters. Sometimes these dreams come to us gently, and sometimes not.

An interesting aspect of the recurring dream is its measuring-stick function. If the recurrence remains unchanged or worsens in content, it indicates that the dreamer, as said, is not addressing the source. She or he could intentionally be ignoring it or could possibly be unaware of it. Once the dreamer takes action, the dream stops or changes to reflect progress and reveal new information. In either instance, after looking closely at a dream signifier, particularly if repetitive, the dreams that follow will almost always give more information and insights.

DREAM 024 - Over a number of years, a man dreamed of flying in jetliners, which invariably but gently crashed, sometimes in almost cartoon-like fashion. These were puzzling dreams, but not frightening.

INTERPRETATION - *In time, the man came to realize that the dream did not deal with his destruction in a real plane disaster. Almost always dreams of disaster and of our deaths are symbolic, not literal. Also, in these dreams, the planes landed intact and cartoon-like, and the mood was not tense. These recurring dream themes dealt with (1) his foolish fear of flying and (2) a lack of direction in his life, which prevented his lofty or higher goals and aspirations from soaring. When he overcame the fear and began to set and achieve goals, the theme of crashing airplanes abruptly stopped.*

+ + +

DREAM 025 - A woman dreamt various times over the years of the same dream scene, looking out from a hillside onto a beautiful ocean. She had absolutely no recollection of ever visiting the place nor any idea whatsoever of its meaning. After more years of this dream, by chance she told it to her mother, who, surprised, asked her to describe it in detail. Here, it was the mother of the dreamer who said, "Aha!"

INTERPRETATION - *The dream was what the mother had seen when sitting on a seaside hillside during the months her daughter was growing inside her. Sadly, perhaps, the revelation ended the recurring dream.*

+ + +

"Two Moons" and Recurring Dreams

What repeated in "Two Moons"? Among other things whose time has not yet come were roads.
The stats:

- *Number of roads walked down: four*
- *Number of roads in which the unexpected occurred: four*
- *Number of rural roads: three*
- *Number of rural roads in which pure joy or great peacefulness occurred: three*
- *Number of city streets: one*
- *Number of city streets in which the mood was at best neutral: one*

These numbers suggest, for one thing, that the dreamer's life is and will be full of unexpected happenings and of the sudden appearance, disappearance, and reappearance of those with whom she has deep bonds. The dream told her, in effect, that this does not have to be a curse. If seen from the perspective of the Norwegian's stoicism, knowing, and calm, the road becomes an unending series of meaningful and beautiful experiences.

In general and in "Two Moons," roads in dreams tend to be part of the dreamer's journey through life. Those in this dream had good adventuring and good messages.

A final point on recurring dream themes: Remember the passing reference to a train in "Two Moons"? It occurred in a portion of the dream not well recalled, when the dreamer went with the Norwegian to the cabin. Two nights after "Two Moons," the dreamer had a train dream in which the wise woman appeared in the guise of a ticket seller. More later on such dream previews.

PART TWO

DREAM COMPONENTS

What are stunning, frightening, and missing are among countless key dream signifiers that fit into more encompassing dream components. They are useful to look at in every dream and are particularly useful to look at in a puzzling or intriguing dream.

Themes
Settings (including time setting)
Plots (including if-then story lines and flying)
Life-forms (including perspective such as active/passive)
Moods
Odds and ends (including time passage such as slow motion)

For a longer list, see the index.

7 | THEMES

Tracing a theme, once uncovered, through a dream is a fast route to the dream's story and messages.

Themes...

...are the essence of dream interpretation. They provide the means to connect key signifiers and weave them into stories.

Identifying themes may seem difficult at first, but look for the clues.

- Recurring settings, characters, plots, etc. have familiar recurring themes, which always point to something you have not come to terms with or acted upon, as discussed in the last chapter.

- Look to your daily life for themes. Dream joy and unhappiness invariably originate in real-life joys and stresses. A good source of dream themes, then, is what stirs your awake-time blood. If you are concerned about a cold on its way, look for a health theme in your dreams. An obvious list of images reflecting the condition of the body would include food (digestion), the bathroom (elimination, cleansing), and terrain features and other shapes (body parts). Less obvious themes and possible meanings are a vampire (blood), a valentine (heart), and wet insulation exposed in an upper floor ceiling (sore throat).

What health condition might be indicated in the underlined words in the next dream?

DREAM 026 - A dreamer saw two inches of <u>water covering his bathroom floor</u>.

INTERPRETATION - *On awakening and finding his bathroom floor dry, the dreamer knew that his "drainage" was stopped up with constipation. He promptly increased the fiber in his diet.*

+ + +

"Two Moons" and the Theme of Integration

"Two Moons" was loaded with dream themes such as dreamer-male relationships, impermanence and permanence, the unexpected, and integration. Regarding the latter, all dreams in some way move us closer to becoming whole, compensating for selective real-life happenings or non-happenings. They advise, correct, review, rehearse, and otherwise balance off what we overlook, yearn for, forget, and otherwise leave unfinished.

In "Two Moons," integration was the essential theme, what the dreamer learned in terms of the integration of emotions with deep knowing. Her feeling of being scared disappeared at the time of her merging with the wise woman's peaceful composure. Her feeling of disappointment from Charles's sudden disappearance was brief because of her reunion with her two dogs and its emotional high.

In stark contrast, the real-life disappearance of Charles was and has been, to be succinct, not peaceful. The dream did not say she had integrated—the two moons did not merge—but it ended with a dream experience of integration. Dreams guide, we decide.

+ + +

8 SETTINGS

The dream location, one of the best indicators of a dream's theme, sets up everything else in the dream.

The Geographical Setting

Settings have logical meanings:

- A city may suggest something built, a center of activity.

- A store may tell you what's in store for you, hopefully opportunities and rewards.

- Your dream house can represent the conditions of the self (body, state of mind, and life).

- Deserts could indicate barrenness and isolation.

- Egypt may be intriguing or whatever else a dreamer associates with the country.

- A library may indicate something knowledgeable.

However, it is the context of the dream and dreamer, not general associations, that best determines meaning. Oceans may always be profound, but what counts is the nature of the body of water in last night's dream and the dreamer's personal associations with it. For example, was it stormy or calm? Was it a recent bone of contention because it was the dreamer's first choice for the family summer vacation and his spouse's last? Did a tragedy in the dreamer's life occur there?

Familiar dream settings are particularly important. Pay special attention to what it is in your present-day life that draws you to them and to any changes in them. If you dream of an oft-visited house, with or without a known equivalent in your awake life, and the house now has a new second-floor addition, look at what that change could mean. Have you added some new dimension, more openness, more space, expansion, or height to your thinking?

Guess what the underlined settings mean in the following dreams before reading the answers.

> DREAM 027 - A dreamer walks down a beautiful futuristic dream <u>hallway</u> marked for the dreamer.
>
> INTERPRETATION - *The dream shows an important passage in the dreamer's religious life.*

+ + +

DREAM 028 - A woman dreamed of becoming lost in a <u>forest</u> while camping with her boyfriend. Later, a stranger on horseback pointed the way out for her to take.

> INTERPRETATION - *The dream told her that the relationship was temporary (camping, the boyfriend not leaving with her). She was lost and unable to see the true nature (forest) of the relationship because of the vast number of details (trees) surrounding her. A special guide showed her the way out of her dilemma.*

+ + +

A single signifier (a forest location, for example) may have multiple meanings. In this last dream, the forest, though a little hostile and not seen because of the trees, still had a noble aspect. In another dream, however, the forest's nobleness may be lost if it's the nocturnal home of a nightmarish pair of eyes approaching your quivering body. The point is that if you've seen one dream forest, you've not seen them all.

Other basic dream components, besides the setting, are in this dream. The theme, subject of the previous chapter, is a relationship. The plot is girl meets boy, girl loses boy, girl finds way out, and boy is on his own. The cast has a guide, here the classic man on horseback, who appears at critical moments to assist dreamers. His pointing the way out of the forest to the dreamer, without her boyfriend, is definitely something for her to consider carefully, because her dreaming self listened to the rider so attentively. More on plot, life forms, and dream mood in upcoming chapters.

What do you think the underlined settings below mean?

DREAM 029 - A dreamer has an inspiring dream of looking down at the Earth from a <u>cloud</u> with spiritual beings.

INTERPRETATION - *This dream reflected the dreamer's considerable psychic talents. What better than a cloud to provide a lofty and spiritual overview from on high?*

+ + +

DREAM 030 - An ambassador, being transferred to a lesser position of responsibility by his foreign ministry, had a recurring dream of a <u>waterfall</u>.

INTERPRETATION - *The dream possibly depicted a fall in position, but given the nature of the waterfall, it also pointed more positively to increasing volumes of activity and responsibility in his career course farther downstream.*

+ + +

DREAM 031 - A family man dreamed of hiding from pursuers, frightened, in a dusty corner of his <u>basement</u>, which in actuality was quite clean. They easily found him, but, before they could get at him, he awoke.

INTERPRETATION - *The dream pointed out the extent to which the dreamer was hiding from family responsibilities, and not very successfully so. Did his choice of dream location also suggest that what was being hidden was something base and neglected (dust), in his deep past, and buried in his subconscious?*

+ + +

The Time Setting

The stopwatch, the clock, the calendar, and the location of important actions and objects are among the dream indicators of time. Look for logical meanings:

- The past may be represented by a younger you, a child, or something behind, below, in back, buried, or to your left.

- The present may have whatever is a focus of the dream near you or in the daily living room or on a ground floor.

- The future could be an older dream version of you, an older person, or something ahead, approaching, above, or on your right.

- Daytime may mean that the theme is clearer and night time that it is more obscure. However, as we saw in "Two Moons," the night can also be extraordinarily illuminating.

There are an abundance of other time signifiers—1945, summer, midnight, May, dinosaurs, a Renaissance painting. Again, look for associations meaningful to you in the context of each dream.

Guess the underlined time signifiers in the following dream:

DREAM 032 - A man dating a divorced woman dreamed that her son showed him a painting that the son was doing of the family. The dream painting then <u>receded into the distance</u>, showing an older, portly man as the father.

The portrait father did not resemble the son's actual father or the dreamer.

INTERPRETATION - *The dream suggested that someone else and not the dreamer would figure in the family picture one future day. And so it happened.*

+ + +

Setting - Vehicular and Other Transportation Modes

Another class of settings is when the dream action takes place on, in, or around things that can move you along. These include trains, buses, a Jaguar (eight cylinders, zero hearts), a jaguar (zero cylinders, one heart), wheelbarrows, and flying saucers.

DREAM 033 - An employee, unhappy about being transferred by his employer to another city, dreamed of buying a <u>train</u> ticket to that city.

INTERPRETATION - *The dream confirmed that he, in fact, finally had his train of thought on track to fully accept the new assignment, which, as it turned out, involved training classes.*

+ + +

DREAM 034 - A man dreams of uncomfortably driving a <u>bus</u> instead of his car.

INTERPRETATION - *The dream told the dreamer that he was hauling too much weight around and on a fixed course in terms of his caloric consumption routine. He got the message and went on a diet.*

Setting - Others

Other types of dream settings are legion: terrain, weather, natural disasters, under water, unknown planets. Look for associations, general and specific, that are meaningful to you.

"Two Moons" and Its Time Settings

Dream time is simultaneous, encompassing our Earthbound chronological time and much more. Dreams frequently mix the past, present, future, and the timeless. In dreams, we can appear as we are or in younger or older versions, finding ourselves in a setting from our childhood or a previous century. We can have dream chats with relatives and friends who passed away years ago. Non-time occurs as well, when, for example, we're trapped in a menacing fog or are chased by a nightmarish something and may have no inkling of the month or century nor care.

"Two Moons" has many examples of this mixing. The dream began in present time, with the dreamer and Fred hitchhiking in the city. But this opening scene had the future too. Fred was somehow left behind at the intersection in the dream and in a divorce later in real life.

The dream next entered a suspension in time for timeless or ageless wisdom from the Norwegian.

The dreamer then returned to current time, meeting Charles on the road as she had many times in real life. The future was here too. Charles passed away two weeks after he faded from the dream.

The last scene had the most time settings. Enjoying the return of the deceased dogs was from the dreamer's past, something she and Fred often had done. Playing with the dogs, who she knew had died, was time suspended or, depending on your belief system, a future time when they may be reunited in the Afterlife. Was the return of Fred at dream's end also a sign of a future getting together sometime down the road? More on this and the future later.

+ + +

9 | PLOTS

The plot structure and the bare-bones story line may point to dream meanings.

The Plot Structure...

The plot structure may contain the breakthrough clue to a dream message. For example, a dream's if-then situation reveals that if you do this, then that will happen.

Plot Structures

If-Then, Then-If, Because-Therefore
Beginning-End, Beginning-Middle-End
Situation-Option-Consequence
Anticipation-Happening
Problem-Cause-Solution, Problem-Cause, Problem-Solution
Passive-Active, Active-Passive, Active-Active, Passive-Passive

Which plot structure is in the following dream?

> DREAM 035 - A woman, pondering over buying or renting a home, dreamed of owning a house with a roof that leaked.
>
> INTERPRETATION - *The plot structure has an if-then sequence. If she buys a house, then she, not a landlord, would be responsible for roof maintenance. The dream didn't say buy or rent. It only asked if she wanted the*

responsibility that comes with home ownership. The dream also told her, whether she buys or rents, that she would be well advised to first check the roof for leaks.

+ + +

Actions - Basic Story Lines

Writing out the basic plot may assist dream analysis. This is particularly true for the ending. What was and what wasn't resolved may help you figure out the message. Waking up before a dream dilemma is resolved could mean its real-life counterpart also has not been settled. In dreams of two or more scenes, no matter how seemingly different, weave them together into a single mini-story. They are always related.

Action words describe the essential plots of dreams and dream scenes. Let's look at one in detail.

Flying like Superman in dreams is a sensational phenomenon, not uncommon, and occurs more frequently to some than others. It can be sheer dream-time fun, the celebration of a success, or the expression of another awake-time joy. Your flying height, prowess, mood, etc. may measure the degree of achievement. Another possible meaning is escapism from the content of a dream and the dream's real-life source. Flying may provide a helpful overview of a situation and a sometimes welcomed temporary withdrawal from being caught up in a complicated one. Clues to the meaning of your flying dream may be found from the nature of:

- Your flying companions
- The terrain and whatever else you were flying over
- What you were fleeing from and fleeing toward
- The plot at the time you went airborne
- Your dream moods
- Associations with recent happenings in your awake life

DREAM 036 - A dreamer enjoyed slowly flying near ground level through a beautiful forest. The trees began to thin, a bright sun lit up clearings, and then he stopped at the edge of the forest. In the far distant haze, across an empty plain, he saw a large crane and two pieces of the framework of a building under construction. The faraway pieces appeared as two long thin lines, a vertical one crossed well below its mid-point by a horizontal line considerably longer. He was awestruck.

INTERPRETATION - *The dream told him that a years-old book project was at last under construction. It promised to be spectacular, particularly in its balance and flow between its support structure (vertical line) and its more voluminous content (horizontal line). The flying reflected his real-time exuberance over having the project under way.*

+ + +

The following are other basic plots and some possible meanings:

- Being chased = attempting to get away from or avoid something feared or troubling

- Losing something = a warning of a literal loss of something now or in the future; a loss of values, identity, or what the lost object symbolizes

- Being lost = being disoriented, off your path, without direction, in an unknown or unfamiliar situation, unable to find a way out of a situation

- Finding things = finding value in what is found, literally or in the symbolic meaning of what was found, such as a belief, situation, or attitude

- Falling = heading for a fall, a demotion, financial loss

- Not prepared = literally unprepared for an exam, etc., feelings of inadequacy

- Nudity = a feeling or fear of being exposed to the cold, to scrutiny, of being found out, of revealing something hidden

All of the above have possible literal interpretations. A falling dream could warn you to pay more attention when hiking to avoid a physical fall. The dream mood is critical to meaning. For example, dreams in which there is no embarrassment over nudity may mean no fear of exposure, an absence of inhibitions, or an exhibitionist bent.

A dream of losing and finding:

> DREAM 037 - A woman dreamed of pulling silver dollars out of a sandbox. Then, in a series of misadventures, different people, including a kid, conned or cajoled her out of them all. At the end of the dream, sad and depressed, she returned to the sandbox, but immediately cheered up when she discovered more silver dollars buried in the sand.
>
> INTERPRETATION - *The dream told her that she had abundance in her life. There were always more dollars and more joys to be dug up from an infinite source. This is like the unending happiness of a child whenever she returns to play in a sandbox, or perhaps what actually happened in the dreamer's childhood and the joys found at the beach.*
>
> + + +

"Two Moons" and Its Variation on the Girl-Meets-Boy Plot

<u>*Placing Loss in Perspective – Plot Structure*</u>

What message clues are in the plot structure of "Two Moons"? It was a Problem-Solution dream, or, more specifically, the following:

- *Problem of Loss*
- *Problem of Loss*
- *Problem of Wither*
- *Solution*
- *Problem of Loss*
- *Solution*

Problems of loss appear to drive the dream. The first loss was of Fred's companionship. It quickly mushroomed into a deeper truth and a much more frightening loss of self. Then, the Norwegian came with the solution! By following the wise woman's example, the dreamer found herself, and all was well. Ironically, two other previous problems remained unresolved: she still didn't know the whereabouts of Fred or how to get to New London, a city near her childhood home. What had changed, thanks to the Norwegian, was a shift in the dreamer's attitude, and the two losses were no longer of consequence.

Then, she was hit with a new problem, the dream's fourth in this count, the loss of Charles. This time, the negative impact, the disappointment, was brief, because, as said, she had no time to linger on it. Within moments, the dream's finale a little farther down the road literally exploded upon her. The old Fred of good-time adventuring was back, as were her deceased dogs.

At this point, the dream's universe integrated. The dreamer merged with her two "girls," who symbolized the double moons, her separated but united two feminine aspects of Feelings and Knowing. Also, it was a reunion of the dreamer with Fred, temporarily departed, and the dogs, permanently departed. Not only was there happiness, but also a memorable experience and reference point for trying moments in the dreamer's awake life.

<u>*Placing Circumstances in Perspective – The Story Line*</u>

Writing out the basic plot: Girl is with but then leaves First Boy, Girl meets Mentor, Girl meets Second Boy (her True Love) and then loses him, Girl re-meets First Boy and meets Dogs.

What does this exercise tell us? In the form just presented, not much! However, in terms of <u>questions</u> to pursue, it's useful. For example, it allows us to assign responsibility.

> *Why did she leave the First Boy?*
> *She didn't. Circumstances left him behind.*

What was the outcome of the Dreamer-Mentor meeting?
The Dreamer learned of the peacefulness that comes from the application of permanent Calm and Knowing to impermanent circumstances.

> *Why did she lose the Second Boy?*
> *She didn't. Circumstances led to his disappearing.*

So she ended up with the First Boy?

Not exactly. She ended up playing with what she was presented with: the circumstances, namely the Dog circumstances, while the First Boy circumstance and (no doubt from somewhere nearby) the Second Boy circumstance totally shared in the common joy.

Examining a dream's plot structure and the basic story line of dreams of particular interest can uncover new lines of inquiry.

+ + +

10 | LIFE FORMS AND RELATED BEINGS

> In dreams, the characters and others of intelligence are almost always the star attractions as well as a primary source of dream messages.

People, Body Parts, and Related Beings

Your role in your dreams provides a lot of information about where you are in life. Were you in control behind the wheel or being driven by another? Were you participating at all in the dream or distant or even not present and outside, observing it as if projected on a 3-D screen or seen through a TV camera?

General questions to examine in your dream log:

- Were you active, reactive, or passive?
- Were you moving or still?
- Were you alone? If with others, did they help or hinder?
- Were you as you are in life? If not, how different?
- Were you present or not present, observing through a camera lens?
- What were you feeling?

At one level, everyone and everything in a dream is an aspect of the dreamer. In characteristics and behavior, other people in our dreams, particularly their out-of-character traits, appearances, or actions, could be commentaries on our own. Dreams, it seems, often use the more gentle approach of having others exhibit to the dreamer what, in real life, the dreamer, in fact, is exhibiting to others. So look for reflections of yourself in your dream characters, particularly your friends and relatives. Have there been times recently when you may have been a tad nasty, noisy, or neglectful, as was the neighbor in last night's dream? Could you use more of the kindness shown in the dream appearance of a generous aunt? If you do not honesty identify with aspects of those you know in your dreams, the message possibly relates to them.

<u>Dream strangers</u> may also point out a negative side of ourselves, one that we may not consciously know. Or they may have advice worth considering carefully. Clues on the merit of their messages relate to how you feel about them in the dream, their costumes, and the murky or vividly clear circumstances surrounding them.

A <u>dream child</u> could represent you at that age, remind you of a childhood incident, or be your inner child, the playful and spontaneous you, or an indication you would best grow up. Have an eye out for the age of the child. If around ten years old, recall when you were that age or what you were doing ten years ago, if not ten days, weeks, or months ago. Look for other signifiers in the dream linking to when you were ten, where you were ten years prior to the dream, etc. The child's related signifiers may be important clues to the meaning.

The following are examples of people in dreams:

- A dream policeman could suggest a need for more law and order in your daily activities or that a real-life matter needs correcting.

- An auto mechanic could relate to a body malfunction (in yours, if not in your car).

- A wise dream figure may be worth listening to.

- A singer may mean you have harmony and rhythm or could use more.

<u>Supernatural beings</u> may or may not be friendly. If visited by a frightening dream ghost, what self-created fear could be haunting you from a hidden corner of the mind? Does an evil dream-something reveal a part

of us separate from our otherwise whole self? Take steps to identify and neutralize the nocturnal uglies in the light of an awake-time morning. In contrast, if a happy dream elf finds something, see what value it has for you or consider if it's time for you to start cheering up others, possibly beginning with yourself.

Guess the meaning of the underlined life-forms:

> DREAM 038 - In one man's dreams, his <u>mother and father</u> appear only to fill a certain role.
>
> INTERPRETATION - *They give good advice when needed most.*

+ + +

> DREAM 039 - A man had to stop his car as a street barricade was erected in front of him. Other drivers began to line up behind him, clamoring to be allowed through. The dreamer asked a <u>policeman</u> if he could pass. The policeman only let the dreamer through.
>
> INTERPRETATION - *The policeman allowed the dreamer through because the request was fair. Unlike the other drivers, not only had the dreamer been the only one cut off in the process of placing the barricades, he was also the only polite one. The dream message? Speak out if you want justice and the cause is just. You may receive it.*

+ + +

> DREAM 040 - A young lady dreamed of what she thought to be <u>ghosts</u> making terrifying noises from behind a door. With the greatest fear, she opened the door only to discover a wheezing old air conditioner.
>
> INTERPRETATION - *The dream told her that old fears haunting her from a closed off part of herself would dissipate if she would open her mental door and examine them.*

Creatures

As with other dream signifiers, come up with your own associations when it comes to representatives of the animal kingdom. These are frequent cast members of dreams. Pay close attention to your dream mood.

One common animal dream signifier is our friend the snake. Some possible meanings:

    Ancient people
    Enemy
    Evil
    Danger
    Dishonesty
    Healing
    Lowdown
    Life force
    Male organ
    Medical arts
    Poisonous
    Regeneration
    Resurrection
    Sex
    Slipperiness
    Temptation
    Treachery
    Wisdom

However, as said, the message is in the context of the dreamer and the dream, not general meanings. One person's dream contact with this reptile along with his real-life attitude may have little to do with another's.

> DREAM 041 - A man dreamed of visiting the rundown estate of a lady friend, not known in awake time. Although he saw little of her in the dream, he was asked to dig a one-foot hole in her garden. He didn't know the

reason for the request, but he undertook the task. He uncovered a small, <u>non-poisonous snake</u>, which he killed.

INTERPRETATION - *This part of a longer dream told him that he was going along in his relationships with the opposite sex, without clear purpose and without questioning. This nonchalance was involving him in rundown conditions and meaningless acts. It had not yet become dangerous or treacherous (the nonpoisonous snake), but he would best kill this urge before it did him in. No longer seeing ladies who had such minor roles in his life would prevent him from digging himself into a deeper hole. The dream had a significant impact on him in terms of relationships as well as of questioning unclear tasks.*

+ + +

Body Parts and Related Matters

In dreams that highlight a body part, make general and personal associations meaningful to you. For instance, hair may deal with thinking (what comes out of the head or mind), teeth with talking, legs with understanding (what "stands under" the torso), knees with flexibility, and feet with foundations (what you stand on). Body parts may also have literal meanings and are loaded with puns.

DREAM 042 - A person had a confused dream, not well remembered, that involved hair dandruff, wearing faded and torn clothing, and the opened mouth of a shark!

INTERPRETATION - *The dream told the dreamer to take certain corrective actions, including cleaning up his thoughts (dandruff from hair), resting in order to stop wearing himself thin, and chewing well in order to stop sharking down his food.*

+ + +

"Two Moons" and Charles, a Very Special Life Form

For many a woman, there could be nothing like a good male with whom to share the adventures of the road, and vice versa. In "Two Moons," the dreamer was blessed with two. But it was significant that these two men, and particularly Charles, the great love of her life, didn't speak and were otherwise in the background. Only the women in the dream spoke. Focus was on the feminine, which dominated the content. Feminine signifiers included the dreamer, the Norwegian, the moons, the canine females, night, the number two, which is feminine, as are all even numbers, and the dream's message itself, the integration of two feminine aspects.

But Charles was and is too important to be dismissed. In the dream, it was appropriate that he was present at the near merging of her two selves (the moons), and the person to whom she excitedly pointed this out. In real life, he went much farther than any other to encourage her to take pride in her femininity and, in effect, to integrate what she did not accept with what she did. The double-moon dream symbols spoke truly. It was appropriate that Charles did not see the two moons integrate, because at the time of the dream, the dreamer had not become fully integrated and, since Charles's passing, still hasn't. But then, who of us has integrated our own separated aspects into a lifelong balance? It was also apt that Charles disappeared in the dream without seeing the integration because this is how it happened in real life, apt and very, very sad.

+ + +

11 | MOODS

Mood colors everything.

Your Dream Moods...

...determine if a setting, character, or plot is suspicious, antagonistic, or uplifting. If one directly connects to a real-life mood, it may reveal the source of the dream. In this and other ways, moods are very close to the messages.

In your analysis of dreams, play with dream moods. Link them to similar moods in other dreams and real-time situations. Make note of any differences between your feelings in the dream and on awakening, along with possible explanations. Write down how others felt, including non-humans. The wilder the emotions—yours, another's, and particularly an animal's—the higher the intensity of the dream message.

As in previous examples, the following dream shows the importance of the dream mood:

> DREAM 043 - A man, pointing a handgun, emerged from a bathroom and herded women, coming and going in a hotel lobby, into one corner of a conference-like room. Its walls were bare. The gunman showed no feelings. The women went complacently, but continued to chat, emotionally unaffected by the gunman and otherwise ignoring him. The dreamer, low-keyed himself, neutrally observed this off to one side, but was surprised by the illogical behavior of the participants in what apparently was a hostage situation.

INTERPRETATION - *The dream told him that the dominating masculine part of his Self was Work (the gunman). Work had hustled his multiple Play selves, his feminine aspects of feeling and spontaneity, into a separate place, out of the action and without adornments. The entire dream cast was surprisingly indiferent, and, in real life, so was the dreamer. He was aware that his feelings were being held hostage by a heavy work schedule, but he was doing nothing about it.*

+ + +

"Two Moons" and Moods on the Roads

Mood interprets. If the mood of the dreamer is awesomely happy, so invariably is the rest of the scene. In the finale of "Two Moons," the dreamer was ecstatic, and so was everything else: the night sky, the landscape, Fred, and the romp with the dogs.

Correlations reveal a good deal about dream messages (for instance, the relationship between moods and roads). As mentioned earlier, the contrast between her neutral mood on the city street and the peacefulness-then-joy on the dream's rural roads is striking. It suggested that her happiness lies in Nature, the spiritual, and road companions of like mind. Therefore, it will come as no surprise that the dreamer is an <u>aficionada</u> of country living and walks in the wilds.

There is a message here for all of us. Should we forget what we love (in dark times, for example), memorable dreams like "Two Moons" remind us.

+ + +

12 | POTPOURRI

Key signifiers can jump out at us from among the odds and ends that compose the bulk of dream images.

Dream Potpourri

A color, number, prop, direction, or other dream potpourri, at times, can break a message out from a dream. It's often easy to spot the whistling purple teapot. The trick is to understand its meaning. But practice, practice, practice. Associate. Give logic and imagination free rein.

In quantity, odds and ends are without end. Engage with us on the six categories that follow. They may have use later when you run across them and their zillions of brothers and sisters in your own dreams.

Props

Clothes

Clothes protect, hide, and disguise, but they also give us data about the wearer. Describe the dream clothes and see what messages are in your descriptions. What do new, faded, full of holes, spotted, mismatched, or stylish clothes have to do with the real life of the person in those clothes? Do they tell the wearer's profession? Do they reveal that your dream is a costume piece from a past century? Do they emphasize a particular body part? A vivid color? What personality characteristics do they reveal? Does a change of clothing in a dream suggest it's time for a new look?

Make obvious associations—hats with the mental and shoes with basic foundations and beliefs. Look for personal associations, and don't forget plays on words. If they stand out in a dream, check to see if you want to "skirt" a real-life issue, "coat" it (i.e., cover it up), or simply "watch" it. Consider a link between a loose dream belt, which catches your eye, to your engine's noisy fan belt or to how your diet is coming along. The following are some other personal associations with belt:

- Punishment and discipline – Were you "belted" in your youth?
- Thrill or success – To "belt" a homerun out of the park.
- Practical or essential – To hook keys and other tools of your profession to.

Food

Food may be literal (for example, suggesting that you should consume more or less of this or that). More often it is symbolic.

What meanings do you see in the underlined?

>DREAM 044 - A dreamer dreamed of a long search for <u>water</u>.
>
>INTERPRETATION - *The dream told the dreamer of a need to drink more water. On another level, it spoke of a need to take in more affection and feeling (water) from loved ones.*
>
> + + +
>
>DREAM 045 - A dreamer felt great happiness in a dream of bringing home <u>Thanksgiving groceries</u> to his parents.
>
>INTERPRETATION - *Seeing his father, who had passed away several years before, led the dreamer to give thanks to good family times in the past, good times that could be recaptured today in dreams, memories, and thoughts.*
>
> + + +

DREAM 046 - Within a week's time, a dreamer experienced recurring food themes on <u>cheese</u>, <u>milk</u>, and <u>meat</u>.

INTERPRETATION - *The dreams told the dreamer to add more protein to his diet. For a protein fanatic, the same set of dreams might suggest that a protein cutback would be beneficial.*

+ + +

Colors

Colors in dreams, especially unusual hues, enhance the importance of dream images and color their meanings.

For important signifiers that puzzle, consider how their colors impact on you, in the dream and in awake-time. What's your reaction to a notable color? What associations do you have with it? Where have you seen it recently? How did the color (shade of green, for example) affect your mood in the dream and now, after awakening?

As an example, take the color of a dream dress that seems a key to understanding. If important, we might also look at the dress's cut, texture, composition, size, weight, specific density, and at whatever the person or thing in it may be doing. A key signifier is a key signifier, deserving our attention. But here, we focus on its color.

Does the black dress bring to mind death or depression? Does it highlight the devastatingly beautiful skin of the wearer? Is a dress of brown suggestive of the earth or of something boring? Is the yellow dress of a sickly or brilliant shade? Is the red one alive with energy? Does it remind you of spilled blood? Is the white one purity itself or devoid of color?

DREAM 047 - A woman dreams of a <u>beautiful white light</u> entering through her bedroom window.

INTERPRETATION - *The dream told the dreamer that a great truth would soon be revealed. It was.*

+ + +

DREAM 048 - A man dreamt of falling into the water in his <u>dark-green</u> business suit.

INTERPRETATION - *The dream made an incisive commentary on his office romance, telling him that it had been a real emotional (water) experience, and a rapid fall, leaving him all wet. It had also been a growth (green) experience.*

+ + +

Directions

Up, left, and downhill may have literal meanings. If you live in the northern hemisphere and dream of going south, is there a health reason to go to warmer climes?

More often your dream's directions are symbolic. Did your dream elevator take you up to progress and higher realms? Did you spend the dream night driving on a meandering highway with no straight or direct stretches? Is the left fork incorrect or one leading to your past? Directions—how things relate to the location of the dreamer—may have telling comments.

Guess the meanings of the underlined words in the next two dreams, both with an up direction.

DREAM 049 - A teenager dreamed of watching the beginning of his high school graduation ceremony. Then he <u>turned his back</u> on it <u>to climb</u> a large number of stone steps cut into the side of a mountain. On reaching the top, he saw a magnificent ocean and a white sandy shore <u>far below</u>.

INTERPRETATION - *The dream predicted that he would undertake a long climb in life alone, without ceremony, and by abandoning honors and public recognition. He would end up at his mountaintop with wonderful personal fulfillment and with a spectacular over-*

view of what his effort, in the end, allowed him to comprehend and appreciate.

+ + +

DREAM 050 - A bachelor, accustomed to stepping out on the town, found himself in a dream climbing a staircase that was built outside, unattached to any other structure, and that eventually <u>disappeared in the air</u>. Several ladies of the evening stood on various steps.

INTERPRETATION - *Did the dream suggest that his pursuit of casual acquaintances was not attached to the rest of his framework and was taking him up a stairway to nowhere?*

+ + +

Numbers

Numbers come in common and uncommon ways (for example, a three written on a dream blackboard or the three cows grazing atop your roof). Numbers have multiple meanings and can be impossible to understand. Pay attention to personal ones, such as your lucky number or the day of the month of your birthday. Try to see how they fit into the dream.

Among the many possible meanings of 175 are:

> January 1975
> 175 Elm St.
> Page 175 of last night's bedding-down book
> Dream No. 175 in your log
> A $175 price tag
> The 175 part of a zip code, social security number, or phone number

Among the many meanings of two could be:
> 2 a.m. or 2 p.m.
> Something to happen in two days, two weeks, etc.

Something that happened two days ago, two weeks ago, etc.
The second day of the upcoming month
Your daughter's age
Something that happened when you were two
Twins
Duality
Combination
Division

Numbers, you may conclude, are next to impossible to decipher, especially at the time of the dream. This may be so. Therefore, if a number seems possibly important, spend a few seconds to see if something meaningful strikes you. If so, write it down. If not, underline the number and review it from time to time.

>DREAM 051 - The number 26 in Dream 25 of his dream log quickly became clear to one dreamer.

>INTERPRETATION - *It meant that he should look at his next dream. Dream 26 turned out to be a repeat of Dream 25's dream theme, only this time, he could clearly understand the message.*

+ + +

Motion or a Dream's Mile-Per-Hour Rates

Another aspect of dream time is the rate of motion of your key dream signifiers. Describe the rate and see what meanings apply to your own life. Examples are "slow-motion," "speeding up," "paralyzed," and "in the fast lane." Instant disappearances and appearances could suggest such things as a quick-change artist at work, a break in your perceptions, an immediate change dead ahead, a changeable nature, the impermanence of life, or an important link between the before-change and after-change things.

>DREAM 052 - A dreamer, warming up for a tourna-

ment tennis match, is in a <u>slow-motion stupor</u>, swinging so slowly he cannot even hit the ball. His opponent is understanding. Through the court screening he sees a beautiful panorama of grassy foothills.

INTERPRETATION - *The dream said that something was not at all working out for the dreamer, in this instance, the way he was handling a self-initiated project. He was in the wrong game, not connecting, not impacting, and very much slowed down. Notwithstanding the goodwill of others involved as well as his own positive attitude, the dream indicated that the easy-going and unstructured approach of a hike in the outdoors offered considerable more promise than continuing the high stress and competitive approach of tournament tennis.*

+ + +

"Two Moons" and Clothes

Clothes appear to have a secondary importance in this dream. The first reference was to a long, dark parka, hood up, on the person first seen sitting in the distance. The dreamer instantly had a lot of information. Parkas suggest an origin from the Arctic or North, the direction of magic, mysticism, and intuition. Given the non-threatening sitting posture, and later, the notable peacefulness of the wearer, the dark color seemed to pertain more to the dark and black colors of magicians and clerics, the mysterious, and the spiritual. The hood covering the wearer's head expanded this perception, suggesting something hidden and mysterious. The length of the parka and its hood also made it reminiscent of the hooded cloaks of monks and ancient sorcerers.

Apparently, it was not cold, another clue to a message. The dreamer did not refer to the daytime temperature, and later that dream day, at night in the snow, she said it was not cold and that she was comfortable wearing light clothing. This would suggest that the hooded parka was less protection against the elements and more a sign of office.

As it turned out, the Norwegian was true to her dream costume. She was from the North, had hidden and spiritual wisdom, was mysterious, and revealed very little of herself. The clothes, however, may not have told the dreamer everything, for example, that the person was a Norwegian, a foreigner, and a woman. A past dream encounter, other dream clues, or an instant knowing may have been at play.

+ + +

PART THREE

SPECIAL DREAMS

Most special dreams differ from mainstream dreams in <u>how</u> they present dream material. Many topics appear in both: family, work, relationships, health, attitudes, and finances, to name a few.

However, mainstream dreams are

- More routine, logical, and practical
- More slice-of-life looks at everyday conditions
- More lifelike, as are their characters, stories, and special-effects
- More low-keyed emotionally, without great happiness or high anxiety, and, at times, without any anxiety
- Less about highly emotional conditions, situations, solutions, and problems, if any

Whereas special dreams, in theme, setting, plot, characters, etc.,

- Are less lifelike, stranger, more bizarre, and gravity defying
- Have more powerful emotions, negative and positive, that can go ballistic
- Have less routine story lines and more danger, chases, surprises, and memorable feats

We do not include some less common special dreams, such as illumination dreams (e.g., meetings with Masters), fantasy dreams (fairy castles, elves), and lucid dreams (e.g., conscious dreams). Our list:

- Anxiety dreams: nightmares, war dreams, and conflict dreams of heavy emotions and trouble

- Historical dreams or dreams of the distant past

- Transition dreams of birth, death, dying, and the dead

- Psychic dreams: ESP, prediction

13 | NIGHTMARES AND OTHER HIGH-ANXIETY DREAMS

> High-anxiety dreams not only point out heavy-duty problems, but also point toward their solutions.

Nightmares...

...are extreme anxiety dreams and can be quite traumatic. Persistent nightmares require particular attention.

There are compensations. You are awake now. Danger is gone at the moment, at least for most of us. Take advantage of the alert. Sometimes the first clue that something is amiss is received through our dreams. Nightmares could suggest that you have been ignoring or not addressing kinder messages of a problem, in dream-time or awake-time. Take some satisfaction that the nightmare could have been considerably worse, in light of the awesome creativity of the subconscious.

When you take countermeasures, they likely will begin to turn down the volume. So don't watch and wait for them on the dream terror channel, where fright controls you. Switch your perspective to the detective channel, where you use your energies to find the nightmare's origins, then confront and eliminate them.

It is here that we begin.

Identification

The first step is to hit each ugly nightmare over the head with awareness. What monsters have you allowed to creep, storm, flood, and charge into your life? What fears, what suppressed negative thoughts and emotions do they represent? Recognition of their sources itself can have nightmare terrors on the road to disintegration. Progress in this regard may be reflected in subsequent, less troublesome dreams.

Fear is a common sources of nightmares. It is said to live in the future, in the world of what might happen. Granted, if the dream lion chasing you is one foot behind, the future is very close to now—closer still if the dream anaconda has just cut off your breathing or if you fell off the 2,000-foot cliff zero point five seconds ago. There are nightmare times when your options appear but two: to die screaming or die silently. Nonetheless, choices are generally broader and allow you to have some control. We have <u>some choice of response</u> to what life puts in front of us (for example, to govern ourselves by constructive action or by fear).

So, let's temporarily freeze-frame the lion, the snake, and the fall in order to look more at nightmare causes. Possible fears include:

- Common (of poverty, rejection, loss of love, ill health, childhood)
- Obscure (of the dark)
- Uncommon (of dining room tables)
- Seemingly reasonable (of an escaped tiger from a circus)

Some potential sources of nightmares deal with non-fears, albeit with fear elements, such as:

- Anger
- Anxiety
- Annoyance
- Bitterness
- Depression
- Disappointment
- Jealousy
- Indigestion
- Lack of forgiveness
- Nervousness
- Poor self-image
- Suppression
- Warnings about health, etc.
- Working off negative emotions built up in the day

Termination Options

If not clear on the source and what to do about it, work more. Dedicate a page in the back of your dream journal to possible associations with your nightmares. Visit the page often after awakening to analyze rather than start thinking about them before sleeping. Talk to others. Read a book on the subject. Possibly seek professional advice.

It is important to refocus energies. Whether or not you've identified its source, if a nightmare has you paralyzed, panicked, or paranoid, consider changing your thoughts. It is said that a thought precedes every emotion, with buried thoughts triggering automatic emotional responses. So think about positive reactions that begin to end the nightmare's power over you.

During the dream, if aware that you're dreaming, consider confronting the nightmarish lead star directly rather than trying to wake yourself up. Ask it to go in peace. Imagine that it does so. For the bold, hug it, find out what it is, and ask for a gift.

If you, sprawled panic-stricken on your living room dream rug, are about to be run over by a charging elephant, take a deep breath, shift attitude, and consider such options as the following:

- Reason. Tell him that you created him out of your imagination and that you can destroy him, so he would best go in peace.

- Humor. Tell him if he doesn't stop charging, you'll take away his credit card.

- Hardware. Conjure up a laser gun, wand, cross, the neighbor's German shepherd, and let fly.

- Boldness. Ask what he represents. Then convert him to an ally for the next adversary that interrupts your peaceful night's wanderings.

Other remedies:

- Convert falling dreams into flying dreams and enjoy.

- On awakening, look for the meaning of the dream.

- If bothered by unidentified nightmares, on falling asleep, ask for a dream that <u>gently</u>, repeat <u>gently</u>, explains last night's anxiety dream.

- Write your own ending to the nightmare. Have the "thing" instantly put on a non-nightmarish disguise, switch the negative dream emotions off, have it more civilly explain to you what's behind it, and respond with what you intend to do.

Some nightmare series are not easily dismissed and their dreamers can see no light side. Nonetheless, identifying and addressing nightmares would seem to offer more beneficial results than not doing anything.

DREAM 053 - A man in a long and complicated chase dream raced through city streets until, exhausted, he stopped. His adversary caught up, his wife! She said that she only wanted to say that she loved him.

INTERPRETATION - *He had tended to forget that she did in real life. He had been ignoring her because of increased office responsibilities..*

+ + +

DREAM 054 - A woman dreamed of a giant green bug flying low over a group of people, frightening everyone, including herself. It returned, but this time she reached up to stop it and it turned into a beautiful purple formation, which began to enfold in her hands.

+ + +

INTERPRETATION - *The dream suggested the spiri-*

tual (purple) benefit unfolding after taking action against a pesky irritation buzzing about.

+ + +

DREAM 055 - A woman, who underwent many and often nameless fears, suffered a recurring dream of a man who changed faces, terrorizing her.

INTERPRETATION - *This stopped one night when, in the dream, she threatened the terror with its destruction at the hands of a neighbor who had counseled her to confront it. The face-changing whatever disappeared for good.*

+ + +

Time for your first complete dream from www.dreamlady.com:

DREAM 056 - "Shots From a Truck"

Dear DreamLady,

I dreamt that I was being shot at by three guys from the back of a military truck. Each of the guys had one arm chained to the top roof-bar of the truck. They were kind of like prisoners, you could say. I was driving behind the truck in a convertible with my mom. There was another person in the vehicle as well but I couldn't tell who it was. One of the guys—he was in a green sweatshirt—turned around and pointed a gun at us. He started shooting. That's when I woke up. What does that dream mean?

Terrified

= = =

Dear Dreamer,

Your dream is telling you about your relationship with your mom and about the shots, which guys are taking at you because of it. To understand it more, ask yourself a few questions. In the dream, it is impor-

tant to note who is driving. If your mom had been driving, the dream could have been about some of the things you're going along with because of her directions and influence on you and your life. However, you said that you were driving, so the dream is talking about some of your drives and motivations as a result of the things she taught you and the advice she has been giving you. If you're a guy, your dream will reflect something different than if you are a gal.

Regardless, the three fellows shooting at you in the dream are telling you that the male part of yourself—that is, the active, dominant, direct, thinking part—is restricted. It's as if the active-dominant-thinking part of you has one arm tied behind, hung up, or imprisoned. The military could be a defensiveness, which you've had to adopt, or it could be a protection. It could also be the fighting service that is contributing to the state you're in.

If the guys are in fatigues, it could be that you are tired (fatigued) and need more sleep.

The number three could also be a clue. It could be three people who you know and who are taking shots at you. Or it could be three days ago, or three weeks, three months, or even three years. Three can sometimes mean sex or it could be a symbol for the physical, mental, and spiritual part of yourself. Cars in dreams are symbols for your drives and motivations, whereas trucks have more of a connotation of work and work-related goings-on.

You say there's also a guy in the car with you. This could signify the one male part of you that is not taking shots at you. He's on your side. You might ask yourself who this could be, such as someone you know who's in the same position as you are. He could be helpful to you.

With regard to the guy with the green sweatshirt who takes direct aim at you, you might try to remember the last person you saw who had on a green sweatshirt. It could also be a play on the words "don't sweat it." Green is also the color of money, (green with) envy, growth, and healing. See if these give you clues as to what they might specifically be relating to in regard to your life these days.

If you're a guy, the dream could also be the threat of a military career, especially in these times when war seems on the horizon. This is especially so because the truck is ahead of you, meaning in the future.

Have you been thinking along those lines recently?

If you, the dreamer, are a girl, the questions are the same. Whereas the female part of you is more feeling than thinking, more indirect than direct, more pull than push, you would also want to look and see what is this other militant, aggressive, protective, and defensive part of you that is taking shots at you.

The other question you need to ask, boy or girl, is, Are the military personnel shooting at you or are they shooting at your mother? If at your mother, this may be saying that in some way unknown to your conscious mind, you're trying to get rid of your mother's influence or that you have recently been taking shots at your mother. If so, the reason for the dream is to show you what you're unaware of and help you to make better decisions about the situation.

The fact that you woke up terrified is showing you that this is an important dream and one that you'll want to spend some serious time thinking about and trying to identify the part of your life that it is depicting. As you begin to work with the situation, you'll find that your dreams will change and reflect that you are dealing effectively with the situation.

Keep watching your dreams and learn more. Your dreams will help you build a happy, successful, and fulfilled life.

Please let me know if I can be of further help with this dream or other dreams that come next.

Hope this helps,

DreamLady

+ + +

"Two Moons" and Anxiety Dreams

"Two Moons" was not an anxiety dream. It was an adventure dream and an uncommonly happy one. Nonetheless, it had one high-anxiety moment soon after the dreamer crossed the intersection and before she met the Norwegian. It was when the dreamer was scared, and scared is a nightmare emotion.

It's true that the encounter with the serene Norwegian immediately obliterated the fear. It allowed the dreamer's own higher and wiser Self to cut in. The dreamer recognized Calm and drew peacefulness and contentment from it.

Nonetheless, it is still important to look at even a single negative high emotion in a dream and see what's there. Identify and terminate the source of scary, no? Often, a good place to begin is to ask, "What's the question?" The following is an early one that comes to mind:

Why was she scared at this particular point of the dream? What was different?

Obvious answers, it would seem, are that she was alone, lost, and with nothing friendly nearby. However, these circumstances, albeit sufficient to move more than a few of us into acute panic, were not the underlying cause of her being scared. They were only an excellent setup, in awake or asleep drama, for trouble. In the dreamer's case, the trouble, which fear and the sudden quiet released, was another issue, apparently repressed and seemingly unanswered: her destination in life. Recently, that destination had been on or at least parallel to the path of another male, Fred. Perhaps she had once thought that his path was hers too. But, in this dark moment of the soul, it was obvious that making another's path hers hadn't worked. Her direction in life could never truly be that of another male's, no matter how great the love. Relationships with others are part of the great external impermanence. It was at this point that the nightmarish-like moment revealed a truth that hit her between the eyes. It was high time that she focussed on <u>her</u>

destination, <u>her</u> mission, and <u>her</u> purpose in life. But what was it? Or as she said in the dream, "I didn't know my destination . . ."

Trouble can have a positive side. If it leads you to the bottom-line issue, you have a target, and simply knowing the target often has you halfway to a resolution. This happened in "Two Moons." In asking the Norwegian how to get to her New London destination, the dreamer had, in fact, already identified her destination. It was home. New London literally was near her birthplace. Symbolically, it was where her roots were, her true Self, and where, it is said, the destination of us all leads to. By attaching a label to her fear, in this instance, "destination," the dreamer had put herself on the road to a solution. In no time, not only had her question shifted from what was her destination to how to get there, but she had also found someone to ask.

Pay special attention to good dream questions. There may be many answers, but there's nothing like a good question. Ironically, the dreamer already knew the answer to how to get to New London. It had been repeated to her in this dream, in many other inspirational or quiet awake-time moments, and otherwise naturally sensed countless times in Nature and elsewhere. The problem was that she refused to accept it. The way to her destination, destiny, life purpose, and home was through integration of her feminine nature.

14 | HISTORICAL DREAMS

Dreams of the distant past may be triggered by something recent that relates to it.

Historical dreams...

...or dreams with a historical element relate to eras earlier than our current one. They may take place in an unknown country, a foreign country, or the country of our birth. You recognize the historical element because of such things as

- Activities
- Architecture
- Clothes
- Culture
- Decorations
- Furniture
- Historic personages
- Inhabitants
- Language
- Literature
- Movies
- Museums
- Music
- Paintings
- Population centers
- Religion

Such dreams may take place entirely in a past era (for example, in medieval Europe) or they may bring a medieval desk or other historic object into a modern-day dream. In both instances, historical signifiers provide the opportunity to step back and look at current situations from another point of view, possibly resulting in helpful commentary as well as lessons, more objectivity, and a fresh perspective. Invariably, thoughts or actions in our current lives trigger these past dreams and dream things.

If you believe in reincarnation, the soul undergoing various birth-death cycles, these dreams may indicate past lifetimes or capture an experience someone had long ago. Past influences may help to explain why certain things attract or repel us. If you don't believe in past lives—seeing historic dreams, for example, as imaginative recreating—it doesn't matter. Everyone can view these dreams as a means to see ourselves as composite personalities incorporating distant past experiences indirectly via books, museums, movies, plays, classrooms, etc.

Aspects of historical dreams also apply to dreams of this lifetime's past, when, for example, we return to childhood haunts, a war-time battleground, or a place where we've vacationed. In all likelihood, something recent triggered these dream visits to the past. The stimulus could be a dream, a passage in a book or newspaper, a friend's comment, a current pattern of behavior repeating one from the past, or unfinished business from past years (for instance, a forgotten lesson or promise).

> DREAM 057 - A young man dreamed of the Middle Ages. He and his cohorts successfully defended a European castle from enemy attack. Later in the castle, he attended a mystical ceremony, which had him spellbound and forgetful of security. There, an enemy soldier, disguised as a spectator, swiftly ended that lifetime.

> INTERPRETATION - *The dream warned that the dreamer needed more protection against ill-intentioned influences and that he should not let his guard down. At another level, because he believed in reincarnation, it may have suggested that he should be particularly careful about these influences, because he actually had been done in by one hundreds of years ago. On a third level,*

the dream may have alerted him to an abrupt end of his work abroad when he reached middle age.

+ + +

DREAM 058 - A man dreamed of seeing himself as a long-ago monk and was pleased.

INTERPRETATION - *The dream approved of his newfound interest in monk-like self-discipline after years without it. Did it also suggest a past lifetime as a monk?*

+ + +

DREAM 059 - A teenage girl studying for a college history exam had a long dream conversation with James Madison, who discussed American history of his time.

INTERPRETATION - *On the next day's exam, a James Madison question actually appeared! The dreamer received an "A" and the teacher's compliment that she understood particularly well President Madison and his times. This was a precognitive dream with its knowledge of the future, a transition dream in that the deceased Mr. Madison visited the dreamer, and a historic dream because the dream visitor was from past centuries and his conversation took the dreamer back there.*

+ + +

The following dream has more foreign than historical influence. However, since the dreamer had an unexplained great attraction to France and things French, it may have suggested ties beyond conscious memory.

DREAM 060 - An American woman dreamed of French doors closing.

INTERPRETATION - *The dream indicated that her carefree, ooh-la-la days were coming to an end and a more sedate life cycle would begin.*

"Two Moons" and Historical Elements

No obvious historical elements appeared.

+ + +

15 | TRANSITION DREAMS OF BIRTH, DEATH, DYING, AND THE DEAD

> Dreams of beginnings and endings can be traumatic, but almost always relate to symbolic transitions.

Transition Dreams...

...deal with the two ultimate transition points of our lives. At birth, we transit from the Beyond into our universe. At death, we transit back to the Beyond. Between entry and exit, we may have dream contacts with those who have already exited and, more rarely, may see ourselves dying in dreams.

Birth

Dream of a baby? It could be literal, with a baby on its way. More likely, it's symbolic, representing the birth of a new

- Acceptance
- Career
- Idea
- Love
- Project
- Or something else "just conceived" and "needing nurturing"

Death and Dying

The appearances of death and dying in dreams, in their vast majority, are symbolic, not literal. When such signifiers come, including our own demise, search your life for the symbolic. This could be a transition from one state of mind or thing to another, a loss or end of something once held valuable and perhaps still cherished, or anything else painful to let go of.

Some closures:

- Divorce
- End of a friendship, belief, or religious affiliation
- Graduation
- Loss of a limb
- Menopause
- Puberty
- Retirement
- Twenty-first birthday or other significant birthday

For those most rare of cases in which death in a dream is literal (at least you take it as literal or possibly so), then it may be best to deal with it directly. If presented as a warning, consider avoiding what you are asked to avoid. If dealing with the dream death of someone you know, consider it first symbolic (for example, an alert to a traumatic change coming in your friend's personal life). If you choose to discuss the dream with the friend, be caring and tactful.

Blessings to those who have meaningful conversations and relationships with others and who treat all kindly, positively, and respectfully. In this way, we've done our utmost should our most recent encounter or communication turn out to be our last.

The Dead

If you dream of someone who has died, consider him or her as the memory coming back to you, a dream image often offering guidance. If you wish, consider the dream as actual communication with those on the other side. Such dreams do suggest the continuation of something after death.

Again, it is less important how you define these dream images. Instead, because they come so dramatically, weigh carefully their applicability to your awake life. Exiting transition signifiers include:

- Hallways, bridges, stairways, a crossing or crossroads, rivers
- The color black
- Aces and eights (a poker hand)
- Broken mirror
- Funerals, cemeteries, coffins, graves, tombstones
- Midnight, a stopped clock
- Organ music
- Skulls, bones, skeletons
- Visitations from someone deceased

DREAM 061- A man, planning to vacation in Brazil in the near future, dreamed of a passport edged in black.

INTERPRETATION - *He correctly interpreted the dream to say that he would not travel as planned. Sure enough, unexpected circumstances killed that year's trip, delaying it until the following year.*

+ + +

DREAM 062 - A woman who felt guilt over her perceived improper care of her husband prior to his death had troublesome, recurring dreams after he had passed on. In them, he was very upset, in contrast to his lifetime when he had been most pleasant toward everyone.

INTERPRETATION - *An acquaintance suggested that he or his memory was displeased with her extensive grief. She worked on her attitude.*

+ + +

DREAM 063 - Soon, the previous dreamer had another dream. She was in the attic when a dove flew in through an open window and nestled in her hands happily.

INTERPRETATION - *This dream suggested that he or his memory was pleased with her loftier spiritual (attic) thoughts and had come from the Beyond (through the upper-floor window) to tell her that he had now found peace and rest.*

+ + +

DREAM 064 - A man dreamed of finding his close friend George, who had passed away, in a rural Mexican village that they had both visited. Shocked, the dreamer said, "George, you're suppose to be dead!" "Not true," his old friend replied. He explained that he had taken advantage of his presumed death to escape to Mexico, enjoying permanent peace and abandoning the sense of being overwhelmed that he had felt in his previous life.

INTERPRETATION: *Such dreams suggest that an essence of the departed remains in some time-space dimension.*

+ + +

"Two Moons" and Transition

In retrospect, a case can be made that the dream had clues that Charles would pass away. His dream disappearance was sudden and without explanation. It happened when he was close to the dreamer, as opposed to farther down the road. He was standing on the dreamer's left or past side. The number of moons in the sky and the number of weeks until his disappearance from life were both two.

However, at the time of the dream, the disappearance of Charles was not seen as an immediate disappearance from life itself. Possibly, he would fade out of the dreamer's life during some future time-out of several months, or years later, when they went separate ways. There were no real-life indications that this would happen. Further, the signifier wasn't clear, a lot else was happening in the dream, and the females, not the males, dominated the dream content. As for the number two, attempting to interpret dream numbers can be a trying process, as previously discussed, and then often successful only if, later, a relevant dream or happening suggests a meaning.

"Two Moons" appears to have been a rare exception, a dream indicating a literal death. However, with reference to the jammed camera, it did not provide a clear picture or record.

The dream had a second transition signifier, the return of the dreamer's two beloved dogs, who had died some time ago. As often happens when those once close to us in life enter our dreams, they bring important and positive messages. In "Two Moons," the dogs told the dreamer that their permanent essence had not disappeared.

+ + +

16 | PSYCHIC DREAMS

Dreams of extrasensory perception suspend our concepts of time-space and are a fascinating aspect of asleep-time experience.

Psychic dreams...

...go substantially beyond our Earthbound notions of space, past-present-future time, and other aspects of the laws of physics. Elements of the paranormal may be in every dream, such as the following:

- Instant mind-to-mind communication (telepathy)

- Seeing what is occurring elsewhere at the present time (remote viewing or clairvoyance)

- Seeing future events, which later take place (precognition). It's not easy to know immediately after a dream if it contained telepathy or clairvoyance impacting on awake life. However, if you recognize this phenomena and have enough information, sometimes you may be able to easily find out if you had ESP with another.

This verification was easy in one dream:

> DREAM 065 - A teenager dreamed of a skillet falling and awoke to a crash in another part of the house.
>
> INTERPRETATION - *He made his sleepy-eyed way into the kitchen to investigate and found that his mother*

had just dropped a skillet and that his dream was clairvoyant.

+ + +

Future prediction may often occur in dreams, but at the time of the dream, finding the prediction itself may be hard enough, let alone knowing its nature. That is, is it a projection of an unsubstantiated fear, one possibility among several, an if-then possibility occurring only if the dreamer undertakes a dream-indicated action, a probability, a sure-fire prophecy, etc.? In time, it is easier to know, particularly if you record your dreams and periodically look back at them.

>DREAM 066 - A man met a woman at a weekend seminar who looked very familiar.

>INTERPRETATION - *Thinking that she had appeared in a dream, he later went back through his dream log for several months and discovered a dream in which she had appeared, along with a favorite toy of her son, a July date near her son's birthday, and a symbol of her German ancestry.*

+ + +

"Two Moons" Psychic Phenomena, and Fred

Did another prediction appear in "Two Moons" about the dreamer and Fred? Like Charles, Fred also disappeared in the dream, but less dramatically when circumstances left him behind at the intersection. Unlike Charles, he reappeared at the end in a joy-filled reunion with the dreamer and the two dogs.

Three possible meanings for his reappearance come to mind. It was the return of a long-held memory of wonderful shared experiences. Or possibly, the dreamer and Fred will have an actual encounter that captures that mood of earlier days. The dreamer seemed open to that possibility by inviting him to participate, saying, "Let's give them one more romp in the snow." Somehow, Fred was again left behind when the dreamer and the dogs romped, but he very much was on the dreamer's road sharing the scene's joy. Or possibly, they could get back together.

Could it be that dreams of future possibilities (as opposed to other future-prediction dreams discussed in this chapter) do not predict, but simply <u>inform</u> that all is in place or could be one day for such-and-such to happen? If so, the dream leaves it to us and other forces outside the dream to determine what does or does not happen. If so, a count of valid dream predictions might better be a count of valid dream possibilities that manifested.

+ + +

PART FOUR

LAST RESORTS AND OTHER MORE ADVANCED TECHNIQUES

To become a professional dreamer, the following are all you have to do and do well:

- Remember
- Record
- Understand
- Act on dreams

The chapters in this section contain assists for the first three. To act on dreams, see Chapters One and Five as well as the index.

17 | SOME WAYS TO REMEMBER YOUR DREAMS

A list of tips to improve dream recall

Ways To Remember Dreams

Do you have trouble remembering your dreams? You don't interpret your dreams because you don't recall any? Help in the form of nineteen suggestions is on the way.

One method towers over all others:

(1) <u>Intend to dream</u>

That is, wanting, sincerely and passionately, to recall your dreams may be the only technique you'll require to awake most mornings with a dream for your journal. If you really believe that your dreams are valuable to you, and if you're good to them, they will, in their own fashion, be good to you.

For reference purposes, eighteen other ways follow:

(2) <u>Suggest</u>

- Program a dream.

Write down one short suggestion followed by ". . . and I want to remember the dream on awakening." Word it however you wish, though consistency may be your ally. The following are examples:

- I want to remember a dream on awakening.

119

- I want a dream about _____ and I want to remember the dream on awakening.

- I want a dream that explains last night's dream more gently and I want to remember the dream on awakening.

- I want a dream that helps me to _____ and I want to remember the dream the next morning.

Then close your eyes and relax.
Take a few slow, deep breaths.
Think your suggestion three times, or fall asleep repeating it. (You can also repeat it at various times during the day.)
Address it according to your religious or other beliefs, or don't address your suggestion to anyone as written above.
In the morning, record a dream responding to your suggestion. Or perhaps the following morning or two. Look carefully for answers in dreams that you remember. However, if there's no success after several programming sessions, continue to keep an eye out, but accept that your subconscious has other plans.

- Pray or meditate.

- Listen to a commercial dream-recall self-hypnosis or suggestion tape. Visit a reputable hypno-therapist or other appropriate therapist.

- On retiring and when drowsy, sip from a glass of water from your bedside table while thinking that on awakening you will sip again and recall a dream. That's drowsy, suggest, sip, sleep, awake, sip, recall, and record.

- Tape "Think Dream" cards in your car, workplace, kitchen, etc. to remind you to recall your dreams.

(3) Avoid

Avoid heavy late-night meals, exhaustion, sleep deprivation, excessive consumption (e.g., non-prescription drugs, booze, sugar, caffeine), and other possible inhibitors of dream recall.

(4) Practice a ceremony

As discussed, make going to sleep a ceremony. Review a past dream in your journal, adding new insights. Place the journal, opened to a new page, and pen within easy reach. Program a dream if you are into direct suggestion.

Make awakening a ceremony. Immediately on becoming conscious, keep the eyes shut and spend several quiet moments on being acutely aware of dreams or, if none, of your feelings and your first thought. Then, open eyes and write these impressions down.

(5) Open yourself to post-awakening awareness

Be alert during the day for spontaneous dream recall, particularly during the morning hours. Your dream memory could be triggered by a spoken word, a song on the radio, a thought, or your image in the bathroom mirror. If, for no apparent reason, you become depressed or inspired, a dream not consciously recalled could be the cause.

(6) Share

Acquire the habit of discussing dreams at the breakfast table, around the office water cooler, or during phone conversations. Such interest in dreams could stimulate you to recall more.

(7) Ingest lightly

See if drinking herb tea, warm milk, or something else soothing or a little sugary just before retiring has an effect.

(8) <u>Eliminate the block</u>

Go after what is repressing your dream recall. If some beliefs are at work, consider suspending them for a trial, baby-step effort. If some acquaintances discount your dream interest, confine your dream talk to dream aficionados. If you have a hidden fear about better knowing your inner self, courage! If you have a fear of nightmares, courage! Also, re-read Chapter 13.

(9) <u>Take dream action</u>

<u>Act</u> on your recent dreams. Review one on those mornings without a recalled dream and assign yourself a dream-implementation task. Action on a dream issue often generates remembered dreams that give you feedback on your progress, particularly if the issue has been the subject of a series of recurring themes. These new dreams may also have insights for future action.

> DREAM 067 - A male dreamer, who found himself with a malfunctioning oversized gas furnace in his living room, was pleasantly surprised to find a repairman at his door to fix it. He was even more pleased, moments later, when several more repairmen arrived to work on other household problems, first stopping to give friendly suggestions to the furnace repairman.
>
> INTERPRETATION - *The dream said that beneficial internal adjustments were underway to regulate the temperature in the dreamer's physical body (house) during a winter cold spell.*
>
> ACTION - *The dreamer began to make a number of external temperature adjustments (e.g., turning up the house heat, ice packs, heating pad) to treat several ailments. He did not recall another dream until five days later, when a celebratory dream adventure confirmed*

that he had taken sufficient action on the previous dream.

+ + +

(10) <u>Educate yourself</u>

Learn and read more about dreams. Catch a talk show on dreams or visit a Web dream site such as www.dreamlady.com.

(11) <u>Obtain fancier recording equipment</u>

Convince your subconscious that you want more recalled dreams by jazzing up your dream-support apparatus. Buy an elegant commercial dream log and a pen with an attached light. Or go to sleep next to a tape recorder and tell it your dreams. Unfortunately, you may find that it takes too much time to transcribe the tapes and that volunteers are not to be found.

(12) <u>Use a pyramid</u>

See what happens if you sleep under, in, or over a scale model of an Egyptian or Mayan pyramid.

(13) <u>Try different positions</u>

Experiment with different sleeping positions (e.g., curled up, on your back). Even better, sleep in a north-south direction, with your head pointed north. If that doesn't work, see what an east-west orientation or a one-minute headstand every day does.

(14) <u>Chart your dreams</u>

Establish the relationship of your dreams to the moon's phases, the north-south orientation of your body, your mental-emotional-physical cycles (biorhythms), your mood on retiring, your state of exhaustion, the time between supper and going to sleep, etc. If you learn that dream recall is best when the moon is full, for instance, go to bed early those nights. Use any patterns to your advantage.

(15) <u>Sleep long and late</u>

An apparently common phenomenon is that an extra amount of sleep over and above the body's minimum requirement for the night is when dream recall is maximized. The last dream of the night's sleep cycle is most likely to be remembered and may also be the longest. So if there's time and the body's willing, after awakening, fall back asleep.

For the Desperate

Nothing worked? Then time for the big dream guns.

(16) <u>Ingest more heavily</u>

Eat immediately prior to sleep (for example, pizza with everything on it). Other nights, one at a time for starts, eat something salty or with a hefty sugar content. Drink a large quantity of liquid moments before bedding down. These gastric feats may provoke several awakenings during the night and perchance a dream recalled. Grab your journal and pen on the way to the bathroom. Ignore suggestion seven above. If your dream is a nightmare, you'll recall, in Chapter 13, that we suggested that one of the sources of nightmares may be what you ate and should not have.

(17) <u>Set the clock</u>

Set the clock to go off every ninety minutes, about the interval between our most active dreaming. The alarm may catch you in the midst of a dream, when recall is strongest. Realize that you may only have a night or three to experiment with adjusting the ninety-minute setting before irritability, hallucination, and other acute sleep-deprivation (if not yours, then that of your significant other) bring this procedure to an abrupt halt.

(18) Sleep with a friend

If all else fails, this is the nearest to a sure-fire remedy. However, understand that it is you who sleeps, not your friend. She or he sits by the bedside in soft light watching for rapid eye movements (REMs) underneath your closed eyelids. After a few REM moments to allow you to enter sufficiently into the dream, the friend awakens you gently and listens to (a) the dream you will inevitably recall and (b) your complaint over its interruption.

If Still Nothing

(19) Be patient

The subconscious is not ready to deliver, at least for now. Allow dreams to come in their own way and time. For the moment, take some pleasure in that many who tend to have better dream recall are the troubled, the stressed, and the light sleepers, not you and other Calm Ones of the Earth.

"Two Moons" and Dream Recall

The dreamer of "Two Moons" is among those who can profitably skim and skip this chapter. She frequently recalls dreams that are vivid in color, content, emotion, and plot.
Why her and not you?

- *Genetics?*
- *A natural as well as practiced curiosity and openness?*
- *Fewer obstacles between her and her subconscious?*
- *An acute interest in stories about herself and her worlds? (What better source than her dreams?)*

+ + +

18 | MORE ADVANCED DREAM ANALYSIS

More than twenty tips follow for unraveling dreams

Introduction

The secret of dream interpretation is to connect the dots—the signifiers, and particularly, the key signifiers. A word, phrase, and sentence in dream descriptions can launch mini-stories. More revealing are images from your own dreams and possibly from what may come to mind on hearing or reading another's dream. From these and other dream perceptions emerge themes, stories, and messages for thought and action.

Understanding what dreams tell us about health, relationships, business, etc. and possible actions to consider is what DreamLady does, much quicker and thoroughly than average. Others, of course, can find and use their dream messages too, a reason why we wrote this book.

Various "dots" have already appeared in previous pages and were connected in actual dreams—underlining key signifiers and coming up with titles, for example. Other critical "dots":

- Links from dream signifiers to awake and other dream experiences (association)
- Dream puns or instant interpretations
- Recurring dreams and dream things
- Dream themes, settings, plots, characters, and moods
- Use of dream mood to understand other dream signifiers

There's no need to connect every dot in every dream. Linking enough to retrieve the essential story suffices. For a humdinger of a dream, connect more.

Advanced Techniques

Attention veteran dream-loggers, dream lab technicians, critics of our back-to-the-basics approach, and readers with undeciphered dreams! Here's a list of approaches for your dream analysis tool kit. Some are old ones elaborated; many more are new.

(1) <u>Underlining and titling</u> (Chapters One, Three, and Five)

An early trick for dream interpreters is to do what Sherlock Holmes did: sort the few important dream clues from umpteen others. <u>Underline</u> what puzzled, stood out, etc. (Step One - Record). Give your dreams the most meaningful title you can (Step Two – Title).

(2) <u>Dream puns</u> (Chapter Two)

Play dream punning with a key dream signifier. Unleash your imagination. What cliches (birthday suit) or sayings (a stitch in time saves nine) come to mind that may relate? What synonyms (bare, naked), antonyms (bare, clothed), homonyms (bare, bear)? What similes (naked as a blue jay) or metaphors (a bear of an appetite)?

(3) <u>What repeats?</u> (Chapter Six)

Dreams can best be understood in a series. What recurs—themes, actions, characters, plots, and locations—helps uncover dream messages. Look closely for what repeats in separate dreams or within a single dream. This increased attention itself will likely produce subsequent dreams with progressively more information.

If you have back-to-back dreams on passivity, the repetition may be a strong indicator of non-progress, inaction, or unawareness with regard to that trait. Check out where you stand. Are you too laid back? Or is the opposite true? Are you too aggressive? Dreams can balance off excessive performance in our real lives. Consider if behavioral modifications are in order.

> DREAM 068 - A dreamer had a series of anxiety-laced downhill dreams. In one she lost her grip and slid down a steep slope into turbulent, cold water. In another, she drove perilously down a steep, curving mountain road.
>
> INTERPRETATION - *Some time later, she dreamed of a peaceful descent into calm waters and instantly knew that she had mastered a big round of life's trials and tribulations.*
>
> +++
>
> DREAM 069 - One long-time retiree has to this day recurring dream settings of his former workplace.
>
> INTERPRETATION - *That setting provides the subconscious dream-generating mechanism with the perfect backdrop to remind the dreamer when his or her current doings become too similar to troublesome shortcomings back then regarding purpose, prioritization, and personal fulfillment. A principle of dreaming is that recurring dreams will recur until resolved. Therefore, unless he permanently shapes up, this dreamer will face periodic returns of this dream location until death, if not beyond.*
>
> +++

(4) <u>Dream mood</u>

Our moods exemplify how dream and awake experience can heavily influence each other. Going-to-sleep feelings enter dreams. Dream moods may last well past awakening. The dream cycle and the subconscious are on a 24/7 schedule. This means that subconscious and conscious minds are continuously and fully interacting most of the twenty-four-hour day, with the conscious mind routinely cutting way back after eighteen hours or so.

Emotions motivate and color our actions and reactions. How we perceive things emotionally seems to dominate how things really are for us. Our feelings go far to differentiate dwellings into well designed, attractive, cozy, too old, too modern, and haunted. Of course, the feelings of one person may not necessarily be those of another.

So pay attention to dream emotions, the dominant emotion, the emotions of others, and your feelings on awakening, particularly if they differed from your dream mood or moods. Glad, sad, and mad are obvious. Kindness, self-righteousness, or not feeling anything may be less noticed.

Ask yourself where you felt the dream mood in awake-time. If threatened in a dream, were you in real life, either identically or in a less exaggerated fashion? If you can make the link between sleep and awake emotions, you may also make additional links between circumstances surrounding the dream mood and the awake emotion. If you do not recall any real-life semblance of that dream emotion, consider if the dream is predicting that this feeling may happen unless you make an effective adjustment.

(5) <u>Give extra attention to the setting</u>

Include the locale (Damascus), the natural or manmade background scenery (forest or ballpark), the weather (storm) and the time (night, 10 a.m., prehistoric). List associations you have with your dream's locations.

Repetitive settings become familiar, harboring longer-term themes often well known to the dreamer.

> DREAM 070 - For two to three months, one person had various dreams of different airports, failing to arrive at each because of various obstacles.
>
> INTERPRETATION - *The series of dreams told him that he had not even reached the takeoff point of a long-pending and cherished goal. After he finally completed*

the first step, other steps followed, a plan took off and his dreams of airports abruptly ended.

+ + +

(6) <u>Find the dream themes</u>

Is the dream telling you about finances, travel, home, school, or work? See if you can sense the trend of the dream. Family, attitude, health, habits, or pets? Often, a recent real-life happening or thought generates the theme. Business, your personality, relationships, diet, history, Nature? Once you have a dream theme, run it through the entire dream, looking for the story that pertains to it.

(7) <u>Ask good questions</u>

Weave the answers into dream messages:

- What's the theme? (As you ask other questions, pursue this one.)

- What plays on words do you spot?

- What stands out the most?

- What was missing or left unresolved?

- What was distorted, exaggerated, or otherwise different from real life?

- Who does the dream person resemble?

- What do other key dream signifiers remind you of?

- What aspects of yourself, perhaps neglected aspects, do you see in other dream characters, particularly in strangers or the exaggerated characteristics of those you know?

- What is the dream trying to tell you?

DREAM 071 - In a dream, an elm tree changed into a peacock!

INTERPRETATION - *The following are good questions to ask: What does an elm mean to you? What do you identify with peacocks? Any dream clues for why your elm changed into a peacock? Some life change on your mind? If not, should it be? Time for you to shift to a showier lifestyle? Or to shift from being a show-off to a more stately person, one more mature, who stands straight and tall? What was your mood when the bird appeared?*

+ + +

If your ex returned in a dream, ask questions. Did she have a real-life message for you? Is something going on in your life now that triggered this visit? Is a similar situation developing in a current relationship that relates to one when you and your ex were married?

DREAM 072 - In part of a longer dream, a woman told her current boyfriend that she was going to see Alan, her ex, about their daughter. The boyfriend told her not to expect Alan to give her any money.

INTERPRETATION - *The dream was about the dreamer's feelings toward her boyfriend and how he compares with her ex. The dream raised questions. Does she now have all that she needs and values? Did she during her years with Alan? Is she missing something by not being with Alan? The dream was telling her to sort out how she really felt now. Everything wasn't perfect with the ex, but neither has it been with the boy-*

friend.

+ + +

A dream ends without a solution. Questions to ask are, What's the problem in the dream that needs a solution? What clues did the dream provide for the next step to take? What is without solution in your awake life? How would you resolve the dream?

(8) <u>Link and link some more</u>

Connect dream images, situations, thoughts, feelings, and other signifiers to their real-life counterparts as well as to past dreams. Also, consider such things as:

- Beliefs
- Current daily life
- Free association (write down where your mind takes you)
- Intents
- Other dreams
- Puns
- The future
- The past
- What you are and are not
- Where you are and where you are not

(9) <u>Look for a literal meaning, then a symbolic meaning</u>

> DREAM 073 - I dream of suffocating in a frightening fog. What are possible literal and symbolic interpretations?
>
> LITERAL INTERPRETATION - *Have you found yourself in a fog that frightened you or caused concern when it closed in on you? If so, what was happening at that time of your life that may be connected to what's hap-*

pening now? Planning to drive through a fog tonight? Did you recently hear about or see fog in a weather report, movie, etc.? How do you feel about fog?

SYMBOLIC INTERPRETATION - *What obscure fears are choking you? What nebulous thing is enveloping you? Describe in more detail your dream mood and find clues in the words you used in your write-up. Was it an undefined, all-encompassing fear? Something unknown? What real-life emotion do you associate with your dream emotion? Did it relate to some insecurity about self or the future? What is hidden in your life or not seen clearly? An important decision, a work situation, a relationship? If you could peer through the mist, what would you like to see?*

+ + +

DREAM 074 - In a dream, a treasured antique clock is missing from the living room wall.

LITERAL INTERPRETATION - *Check to see if it's still there. Did you lock the doors and windows last night? Will you tonight?*

SYMBOLIC INTERPRETATION - *Losing time? Where has your time gone? What or who is robbing it? Where have the good old times gone? Time to appreciate valued friends and things before it's too late?*

+ + +

(10) <u>Seek a simple meaning</u>

Don't overanalyze. Concentrating on the type of beans and their meaning may be fun, but you could miss the more important, basic significance of the story of "Jack and the Beanstalk."

(11) <u>Integration</u>

All dreams may well have elements to make the dreamer whole and to compensate for real-life imbalances. Dreams often present the rest of the real-life story. They can provide the opposite of a belief, counter an action or non-action, or fill in a gap. Dreams can point to what you are not, what you desire, what you have overlooked or forgotten, or what you take for granted.

> DREAM 075 - Someone dreams of being late to work.
>
> INTERPRETATION - *On the one hand, if lateness is the problem, is it because you overslept once? If it's chronic, what are you avoiding that awaits you at work? No enthusiasm for your current job? Want a new one? On the other hand, if you've never been late in ten years, are you too punctual? Obsessed with being on time? Is a manic-compulsive fear of tardiness awaking you at night? Is the dream telling you to take a long vacation and really be late?*
>
> + + +

(12) <u>Think of the dream as a movie</u>

What did the scriptwriter try to say? What did she or he do to emphasize what she or he tried to say? How was it resolved? As you know, you, of course, are your dream's scriptwriter.

(13) <u>Go with your first impression</u>

What you first think of on awakening may well be a valid interpretation and therefore important.

(14) <u>Practice signifier-thinking</u>

During non-sleep time, dream-think. Contemplate things symbolically.

DREAM 076 - A person who had just visited a friend stopped his car to check a map for the route back home. He saw a bird fly overhead back toward the direction he had just come from.

INTERPRETATION - *He thought that the bird was a message of where his heart was at that moment, wanting to be with his friend rather than heading home.*

+ + +

DREAM 077 - A man was sitting at his table watching couples dance under flashing cabaret lights when he had a real-life dream. He saw the faces of the dancing couples become the faces of long-departed friends. Some had passed away, and others he had not thought about for years, but the fond memories swept over him until the nostalgic dance song ended, breaking the spell.

INTERPRETATION - *The episode reminded him of the bond one keeps with good friends.*

+ + +

(15) Think outside the box

Overcome the mental block between you and the meaning of a particularly elusive dream. Turn off your beliefs. Turn on openness and imagination. Try something sane but different that may cast light on an elusive meaning. Does a sketch of the terrain or the twists and turns of a hallway remind you of a part of your anatomy?

(16) Meditate or think not

One way to interpret is to sit in a comfortable chair alone in a quiet place, back straight, eyes closed, all muscles relaxed. Take a couple of deep breaths. Then concentrate only on your specific dream question (e.g., the meaning of a specific key signifier). Let images and thoughts pass across your mental screen. Observe but do not engage. Let them pass on. Then, with eyes open, write down possible answers and meanings.

(17) <u>Look at other levels</u>

Dreams have different levels of meanings.

> DREAM 078 - A dream featured a short near-vertical slope connected to a roof atop a huge, empty storage-like unit open to the air. The slope, part of a hill-like wedge, and the roof were covered by a thick mat of newly grown bright-green grass. Very tall, slender, and fragile-looking metal rods embedded in a massive cement foundation far below supported the roof. A half-dozen high-tonnage trucks and buses were zooming all over the slope and the roof. The drivers were having a ball, showing off outrageously. The dreamer was astonished that the roof and rods not only didn't buckle or sag, but that they didn't even wobble in the slightest.
>
> INTERPRETATION - *The dream spoke to him on two levels, one regarding work and the other his injured knee and lower leg. Specifically, it told him that holding down three part-time jobs was causing little stress to his body. He was working hard, with lots of drives and motivations (large trucks), but without physical hardship.*
>   *Regarding the injury, the dream had presented an X-ray side view of the knee cap (the slope), the area supporting the above-knee weight (roof), new muscle growth (grass mat) from six weeks of workouts on exercise machines, the ligaments, tendons, etc. (support rods), and the feet (foundation). The heavy weights, which he had used for knee exercises, were contributing to a support structure able to handle the load, and the healing process had accelerated. Perhaps the dream also said that, although the knee was supporting well the current load*

ings, he should not overdo them (the fragile-looking rods).

+ + +

(18) <u>Review past dreams</u>

Return periodically to dreams in your journal not sufficiently understood and devote a minute or two to see if new insights have emerged. With the passage of time and the practice of dream interpretation, you may uncover predictions that have since taken place, repeating signifiers to watch for, and additional meanings not seen at first.

(19) <u>Learn more</u>

Besides practicing dream interpretation with self and friends, read and visit Web sites related to dreams.

Last Resorts

(20) <u>Take a signifier apart</u>

Choose one key signifier and have a question-and-answer session with yourself:

- What comes to mind when you think about a specific dream signifier? If a dream glass of orange juice calls your attention, can you link it to a recent experience with the juice? Or to a past dream? Do you associate your like or dislike of the juice to a similar feeling, which you currently have toward a problem or person? What happened the last time you drank some?

- For a very important signifier, describe it more in detail—dull, freaky, tasty, soothing, strong-looking, inspiring. Then go through this longer description to find links to you or to someone or something else.

- Play word association with "orange juice." Undergoing any emotions related to someone named O.J.? Is orange a school color?

DREAM 079 - A man with a sore throat dreamed that his mother flew into his backyard in an orange biplane.

INTERPRETATION -

Questions and Answers With Self

Q: Are we dealing with a literal future landing?

A: Impossible.

Q: Puns?

A: Let's see. To plane (a piece of wood in carpentry, to slide on invisible highway ice)? To travel by air? A geographical or spiritual plain? Something plain and blatantly clear? No, nothing here.

Q: Something from the past (backyard, biplane)?

A: Hmm. During my childhood years, Mom gave me orange juice when I had a cold. Aha! Mom flew in with her tried-and-true, old-fashioned remedy from the past, Vitamin C. Time to pick up and swallow a gallon or two.

+ + +

(21) <u>Role-play</u>

Ham it up with an expanded variation of "Take a signifier apart," immediately above. Position two chairs facing each other. Sit in one as an investigative dream reporter. Ask the dream baby who she is. Move to the other chair and, as the baby, answer the question. Conduct a mock dialogue, going back and forth. For a better variation, have a real person play the reporter.

DREAM 080 - A male dreamer dreams of a baby and a train.

INTERPRETATION -

Role-Playing

Dream Reporter (played by you or a friend): What do you represent?

Dream Baby (played by the male dreamer): Goo!

Reporter: Yes, yes, but speak English.

Baby: Something new, just born, coming.

Reporter: Are you literal, or real?

Baby: No. The dreamer's not pregnant.

Reporter: I know. He's a male. What about his friends?

Baby: Only with his ideas.

Reporter: Moving right along, what specifically do you represent?

Baby: I'm newly alive, in transition. I can bring much joy, but now I need nurturing.

Reporter: What's your relationship to the dreamer's life?

Baby: The choo-choo knows.

Reporter: The what?

Baby: Ask the train.

(The dreamer plays the role of the train.)

Reporter: So, Mr. Train, why are you in this dream?

Train: The dreamer needs more training to handle me, so he can get on track and make the connection.

(22) <u>Tell the dream to someone else</u>

You did this when you role-played in Tip 21. Here are some reasons to do so:

- The message may come in the retelling from within or from the person you tell it to. Pay particular attention to what you previously missed—puns, new emphasis, and new explanations revealed as you relate and the other responds.

- Tell the dream to two or more people and call it group dream therapy. Continually find out if several minds are better than one. Ask them what your dream would mean if it had been theirs.

- Visit <u>www.dreamlady.com</u> and e-mail your dream to DreamLady.

(23) <u>Dream another dream</u>

- Go back to sleep. Each night brings a series of dreams, as many as five or more. This means that your next dream, particularly in the same five-to-eight-hour sleep cycle, may go far to explain a previous one that was not well understood.

- Wait for a dream another night. Subsequent dreams often repeat, in some fashion, the old one's message.

- Or immediately before falling asleep, request another dream to explain more clearly what the previous one said.

(24) <u>Use the dream anyway</u>

Even if there is no understanding, immortalize the dream in a sketch, a poem, or some other kind of artistic rendering.

> DREAM 081 - A woman dreamed of a beautiful butterfly, but never figured out why.
>
> INTERPRETATION - *She nonetheless bought a butterfly pin and placed it on the podium during her speaking tours. It provided her with great strength and self-confidence.*

+ + +

If Still No Satisfaction

(25) <u>Patience</u>

Come back later. Place a hold on further conscious analysis. Give the message more space to come. Trust that, in time, the subconscious will reveal more clues in a future dream, a flash of insight, or a confirmation in awake life.

"Two Moons" and More Advanced Dream Interpretation

It was abundantly clear to the dreamer that the moons on the left and right horizon were significant. They were huge and a spectacular visual. It was their meaning that puzzled.

General associations with the moon, applicable to the dreamer, reinforce other themes in this dream. It is change in terms of its phases and nightly locations in the sky. Its twin forms rapidly moved upward and disappeared along with one of the two people under them. The moon is also constant in that her comings and goings, as those of people, are part of a permanent cycle. In this dream, the moon, in full phase, was at the maximum of her powers, and doubly so because of the two moons. In similar fashion, integration, the achievement of which is the main dream theme, maximizes power.

A multitude of moon-based feminine associations appeared in the dream. These included the <u>dark</u> and <u>quiet</u>, lit up by a glow, <u>cold</u>, <u>reflecting</u>, and <u>passive</u> if not <u>stoic</u>. The moon and the feminine, not surprisingly, are also connected with the <u>subconscious</u>, where lies the <u>intuitive</u>, the <u>instinctive</u>, <u>sleep</u>, and <u>dreams</u>.

Artemis, the moon goddess, loved the <u>woods</u>, <u>wild things</u>, and the <u>chase</u>. She is, therefore, an appropriate persona to look down upon female adventurers on country roads. Artemis is the twin sister of Apollo. The two represent <u>female-male</u> balance, the route to which, "Two Moons" suggested, was through the integration of the dreamer's two separated feminine aspects.

More on these two aspects, why they didn't join, and Charles in the final chapter.

+ + +

19 | DREAM LOG MAINTENANCE

> Consider devoting dream journal pages to improving dream recall, keeping lists (e.g., of people appearing), and quantifying dreams (e.g., by type), all suggestions included in this chapter.

Dream Log Maintenance...

...is for die-hard dream buffs and connoisseurs not yet up to their neocortices in dream journaling. For the rest, skim.

Possible Journal-Enhancement Activities

(1) <u>Conduct a daily review</u>

Systematically review at least one past dream every day. Add new thoughts, predictions, and levels of meanings. Elaborate on old thoughts. Record dream characters, settings, plots, and other signifiers that recurred in subsequent dreams. Draw pictures of an interesting dream image. Use different colored pens or markers for what you add to the original interpretation and date what you add. To more easily track specific dream signifiers, use the same color to underline or highlight what interests—Mom, sports cars, flying, locations, etc.

Consider doing these reviews at the same time each day. The time just before falling asleep has the advantage of revving up the mind's dream-recall machinery. Or review immediately after awakening. If you do not recall a dream that morning, put your dream analysis time to good use. Weeks or years later, a dream may have an entirely different meaning, but one equally valid.

(2) Maintain lists of your dreams

Have a section at the end of your dream journal or in a separate notebook in which you track the dream aspects that most interest you. For example, you could write important numbers (e.g., special dates, your age at pivotal points, zip codes) on a page along with numbers appearing in your dreams and their possible meanings. Over time, patterns may emerge, assisting you in decoding old dream numbers and new ones when they first appear. Similar pages could be kept on animals, vehicles, locations, recurring signifiers, dreams in which you were active and passive, etc. Such a list enabled one dream devotee to see his dream messages as well as the frequency that certain people appeared in his dreams, enabling him to more readily find these dreams.

No.	Date	Title	Friend	Message
403	Nov. 1	Banked Landing	---	If I turn sharply, I'm on target
404	Nov. 2	Elimination	---	Eliminate pending paperwork!
405	Nov. 6	Guidance	Daphne-2*	Let friend

* Her second appearance in his dreams.

(3) Relate your dreams to cycles

Look for correlations (for example, between dream recall and the phases of the moon, a menstrual cycle, or other cycle). Or between dream recall and pre-sleep dream programming, review of an old dream, and consumption. Or between dream programming and the content of the resulting dream. One person discovered that each full moon promised vivid dreaming.

(4) Collect dream lore, etc.

To another back section of your journal, or to a separate loose-leaf notebook, add clippings on dreams, notes from your readings on dreams, a list of dream books read or to read, dream Web sites of interest, interpreting tips that you've found helpful (particularly ones you've found on your own), sketches, dream to-dos, etc.

"Two Moons" and Journal Maintenance

The dreamer of "Two Moons" comes from the same innate interpretation school as DreamLady, having long ago grown beyond any five-step approach. She regularly records her dreams and her thoughts on many of them. She less often titles them. She also uses her journal for poems, inspirations, meditations, and other observations. Years of writing down dreams and interpretations have improved her ability to understand them without the elaboration suggested in this chapter and in earlier ones. She's not above learning more from her dreams by telling them to special others.

This is our approach as well. As you progress in understanding and using your dreams, test, use what works, and discard the rest.

+ + +

PART FIVE

CONCLUSION

What's left before a chapter of DreamLady's interpretations?

- Questions and answers
- Your final exam
- Suggestions for more dream activities
- A pre-dream checklist for nightly checking out of the known world

20 | A FEW QUESTIONS AND ANSWERS

Some questions and answers here, most not yet seen in previous pages

Questions and Answers

Where do dreams come from?

They may come from within (the subconscious, core beliefs, memories, upset stomach, neocortex*), way within (the soul), without (perceived external stimuli), and/or way without (spiritual guide, higher self, Providence, universal forces). Further pursuit could lead us into lengthy, fascinating, controversial, and contradictory directions, but it won't, because our answer or non-answer stops here. Where do you think they come from?

* This is the largest region of the brain and evidently one of the last to be understood. It remains as active in deep sleep as in awake life, but, in deep sleep, all communications with the outside world are apparently cut, suggesting that it and "you" are on your own.

+ + +

What should I do when asked to interpret another's dream?

Be a mirror, a sounding board. Ask good questions. Offer suggestions. Bounce possible meanings off the dreamer (for example, what you find meaningful or what it would mean if it had been your dream). Don't impose your own interpretation. Remember that, in the end, the dreamer is the best person to know which way to interpret the dream. In my response, I give many approaches and dreamers de-

cide what fits or not. If and when something you say makes sense to other dreamers, smile with them.

+ + +

Why aren't dreams in easy-to-understand everyday talk?

Words are too limiting. Pictures are much more meaningful. They contain many more messages, now and for future interpretation. It is a different part of us that understands the beauty of paintings or music. It is this part that communicates to us in dream language, which is mostly images. You read the words "round ball" and they have some meaning. You see a two-dimensional picture in a magazine or a three-dimensional dream image of one and you instantly have dozens more data bits. In a glance, you know its size, color, degree of fullness, roundness, smoothness, what's happening with it, where it is, its composition, what kind it is (beach, volleyball, etc.), who is doing what with it, what or who is nearby, its significance at that moment, and on and on. Some of us learn Spanish in our home or as a foreign language in school or in another country. There's no reason why we can't learn dream language as well as an awake-life one.

+ + +

Isn't it possible once in a while to have a meaningless dream?

No. No dream is too short, too long, too silly, too involved, or too insignificant. The more straightforward the dream, the more we need to look at it.

> DREAM 082 - A man, who regularly worked six days a week and who was not an alpinist, had recurring dreams of mountain climbing. The dreamer dismissed them as sheer entertainment and pure fantasy.
>
> INTERPRETATION - *When a friend suggested the dreams could be telling him to cut loose, go on an ad-*

venture, and work out energies being denied in awake life, the dreamer agreed.

+ + +

What do you tell people who think understanding dreams is nonsense?

It's their choice. What people believe is true for them. We, the co-authors, believe that everyone dreams, although some dreams are not remembered, that every dream has something to say, that ignoring dreams ignores a whole other dimension of the dreamer, and that dreams are the most creative art form going.

+ + +

Can you go overboard with this dream thing?

Yes, for example, in having too much escapism, narcissism, fanaticism, and hypochondria. Do not overdo reliance on dreams.

+ + +

The teacher of a dream class asks: What should I do with students who overdo interpretations, embellishing them with an overlay that misses the soul message?

Some expect too much from their dreams. Work with what is given rather than spend hours on what is not given. Trust yourself to intuitively say "Aha!" and come up with the answer. Tend to avoid interpretations that are too vague, detailed, way-out, or too long as well as too limited.

+ + +

How can I get rid of nightmares and other dreams I don't want?

Hit them over the head until they give up. Three possible clubs:

- *Identify and neutralize the source. Change something*

(for example, your diet or your attitude). Take responsibility for your life. Forgive, understand, have compassion. Live in the present, not past grief or future fear.

- *Accept the now, beginning with who you are, where you are, how you are. If you don't like aspects of the now, change them or laugh and enjoy what you have wrought.*

- *Talk to a professional.*

+ + +

What about dreams of those from cultures outside the USA?

A dreamer's signifiers come from her or his experience, a heavy part of which may be cultural. DreamLady.com, the book, reflects the largely English-speaking and United States cultural backgrounds of the co-authors. A dreamer who grows up in a country without baseball or baseball interest and without other exposure to the game is unlikely to have baseball dreams. However, the principles in the book are valid for all cultures. In some, falling teeth dreams are said to indicate the coming death of someone known to the dreamer. In the United States, teeth dreams may less ominously mean that it's time to see the dentist, that you have been bad mouthing someone, making biting comments, gossiping, or otherwise showing too much teeth. The question for all who have a teeth dream is, What associations do you make with your dream teeth? Something in your awake life at the time of your dream, a past experience, other dreams, and, if it has not already figured, with your cultural heritage?

+ + +

Do some dream in black and white?

Yes. We wonder if they are blocking, not remembering dream colors, or seeing life too rigidly or in too black-and-white a fashion.

Could they *use more color, integration, and more paying attention in real life?*

+ + +

Should I use a commercial dream dictionary?

Write your own. It'll be much better.

+ + +

Why doesn't your book have an alphabetical list of dream signifiers or symbols so that readers can look up their meanings?

See the previous answer.

+ + +

When do I do what a dream specifically tells me?

What do you think? Do you trust the person who said it? Is it caring and not harmful to you or other people or things? Would you do this in real life? Does it feel right and make sense, or is it better not to act? Because a dream message worked out well for us one time does not mean that we should blindly take on faith what our dreams say. They can have elements of make-believe, exaggeration, and delusion. Sometimes they are simply expressions of our fears and should never be taken at face value. We need to use discernment. By all means listen, learn, and do something, if only contemplate. If your heart and mind agree, consider doing it.

DREAM 083 - A professional lecturer dreamed her supervisor told her to gargle a specific chemical solution.

INTERPRETATION - *Because she looked up the chemical and found that it was not harmful and highly respected the supervisor in real life, she tried it. The substance worked, clearing up an accumulation of phlegm that had been handicapping her lecture deliveries.*

If I dream of someone I know, should I contact her or him?

Consider doing so. Perhaps avoid daily phone calls to your mother or another who appears nightly in your dreams. If the dream involves sensitivities, be tactful (for example, not mentioning the dream but simply calling to say hello and chat about each other's doings).

+ + +

Does dream programming block spontaneous dreaming?

Probably. However, your subconscious often strikes back, inserting your dream suggestion into the context of what it already had in store for you in the night's dream adventure, if not outright ignoring it (for the time).

+ + +

Aren't there universal symbols?

There are universal meanings. Mother is a universal symbol, but its meaning depends on the specific dream and the dreamer. Your experience with your mother may be different than mine.

+ + +

What about daydreams and other images coming to us from outside of our dreams?

The approach to understanding dream signifiers works here too. For example, consider images that come immediately prior to falling asleep or immediately after awakening as extensions of your dreaming. Record them in your log. Treat them as regular dreams.

+ + +

What about a dream in which I wake up in the dream only to realize later that I was still asleep dreaming?

Is there something in your being that is really buried and that you do not wish to look at? Did you think you "awakened" from a dream with understanding, when, in fact, you haven't really understood, neither in the dream nor the related real-life situation? Such dreams are very unusual and very special. Give them extra consideration.

+ + +

What does it mean if I am aware that I'm dreaming while I dream?

It means you're having a lucid dream. People with more mind control and a higher state of consciousness, as well as an acute interest in lucid dreams, may have them more often. In mine, I tend to go with the dream content in order to capture the intended message. Others advocate taking command. For example, they fly, they zap the nightmare monster, or better, they ask who it is or hug it and see what it turns into. Whether you're active or an enlightened observer, enjoy. Consider reading a book about them.

+ + +

How do I handle my children's dreams?

I try to interest children in their dreams. I shared appropriate dreams with my children and listened to theirs. It's important to be careful and not get too deeply into their social space. Talk to them with more tact, imagination, and humor than to other folks. Emphasize the positive and the applicability to the child's life. Downplay the negative.

> DREAM 084 - A six-year-old girl dreamed that a hippo swam up to her boat and ate her book. She awoke crying and ran to tell her mother.
>
> INTERPRETATION - *Mom responded, saying, "Oh, but the dream did not end. The hippo said, 'Yum! Yum! You write good books, Chris. What a delicious book!' and then swam away." The little girl laughed and was soon fast asleep.*

How can I tell if last night's dream was about the future?

Wait.

+ + +

What about sex signifiers and sex in dreams?

The question is, What is it telling you about how you see sex? If an eighteen-year-old dreams of a female plumber, he may see sex in some mechanical and fixed fashion. Associate what you see as dream sexual signifiers with your real life. Do you look for a general release from daytime activities or routines? Suffer sexual hang-ups? Do you seek in your dreams to compensate perceived sexual lacks, to enjoy yet more erotica, or to work out inhibitions and repressed desires? Think upon these and other things. Seek integration. Sex is not everything. The dreamer is the only one who knows exactly what this means for him or her.

+ + +

Am I a butterfly dreaming I am a man, or a man dreaming I am a butterfly?

Yes.

+ + +

Now tell me about dream anima (the emotional and intuitive feminine force in men), animus (a woman's discerning masculine force), sleepwalking, hypnosis . . .

Or dream healing, dreaming and brain waves, gestalt (a holistic approach to dream interpretation), numinous experiences (spiritually elevated dreams), dream labs, and dreams in holy books. For these and many more fascinating topics, go elsewhere. Our focus is to encourage you to understand your dreams and use them for your everyday benefit.

+ + +

"Two Moons" and a Question About Previews

What does it mean when you flash on something in a dream that later happens?

These are previews and are common in dreaming. A remark, a thought, a sudden mood change, a glimpse of something, or a noise from somewhere may alert you to what you'll run into later. When they appear, you inevitably know that you and it are going to cross paths. These setups by your subconscious, identical to those by scriptwriters in horror films and other movies, call your attention to something important. In dream interpretation, they point out key contributors to the dream's messages.

In "Two Moons," when the dreamer first glimpsed the figure sitting by the side of the road, she knew that there would be an encounter. This preview led to the Norwegian and important insights on how to deal with life's impermanence. Add previews to your list of key signifiers to interpret.

+ + +

SOME MEMORABLE DREAMS OR YOUR FINAL EXAM

21

Your four final-exam dreams offer four opportunities to compare what you see in a dream to what others saw.

Some Memorable Dreams or Your Final Exam

Instructions:

1. Read each dream, then write your interpretation on the blank page that follows or on a separate sheet of paper.

2. Compare your understanding with the dreamer's on the page after the blank one.

3. Credit yourself if you underline key signifiers and if you find a dream pun and a dream message. Credit yourself for observations similar to the version that follows and, perhaps more importantly, for variations and new interpretations valid for you and possibly for the dreamer as well, even though not in the answer. Assess and learn from what you might reasonably have also come up with, but didn't.

Final - First Dream

A young man dreamed of his friend Linda, with whom he had a wonderful relationship, but one with gaps in its closeness.

Step One - Record (Underline key signifiers.)

> DREAM 085 - I was on a sailboat at sea alone with Linda. It was pitch black. She was steering at the helm in the stern. I worried about where we were going. Linda said not to worry, but I still did. I felt my way along the railing to the bow. A guide suddenly appeared in a glowing white robe and motioned for me to follow him ashore. I called to Linda, asking if she wanted to come. She didn't. Immediately, I found myself in brilliant sunshine. Colors were vivid and enhanced. The guide pointed to a magnificent bright white city on a hill and to a specific house, which was mine. I awoke ecstatic.

Step Two - Title

Step Three - Associate (Write down what you underlined and possible meanings. Guess!)

Step Four - Interpret (Weave what you've written above into a brief story.)

Step Five - Act (Write a possible action the dreamer might take.)

Interpretation - First Dream

Step One - Record

I was on a <u>sailboat</u> at sea alone with Linda. It was pitch black. She was steering at the helm in the stern. I worried about where we were going. Linda said not to worry, but I still did. I felt my way along the railing to the bow. A <u>guide</u> suddenly appeared in a glowing white robe and motioned for me to follow him ashore. I called to Linda, asking if she wanted to come. She didn't. Immediately, I found myself in <u>brilliant sunshine</u>. Colors were vivid and enhanced. The guide pointed to a magnificent bright white <u>city on a hill</u> and to a specific <u>house</u>, which was mine. I awoke ecstatic.

Step Two - Title

"The Way"

Step Three - Associate

<u>sailboat</u> = a spiritual journey

<u>guide</u> = guidance

(change from pitch black night to day of) <u>brilliant sunshine</u> = uncertainty to enlightenment

<u>city on a hill</u> = a spiritual center

(my) <u>house</u> = my place in the city

Step Four - Interpret

I am at sea, in the dark, feeling my way, and drifting in my relationship with Linda and in my life direction. I am not at the helm of my destiny. A guide points to the way to seek in my life, a way that is not with this relationship, if with any. Mine is more a spiritual quest, a path my friend chooses not to take.

Step Five - Act

The dream suggested that I acquire more spiritual direction in life. It told me to communicate better with Linda, work out uncertainties with her, and talk to her about where the relationship is headed. After consideration, I did, telling her the dream. We both benefited.

+ + +

Final - Second Dream

A young woman, married with two children, had this dream.

Step One - Record (Underline key signifiers.)

> DREAM 086 - I dreamed of walking in the desert. I felt relief to be away from home and I identified with the nothingness of my surroundings. Then a man on horseback followed by two others rode up and kidnapped me, sweeping me off my feet. I rode behind this first rider, sidesaddle, frightened. The horses changed appearance to something akin to stuffed stage horses with very hairy legs. I was faced with the dilemma of continuing sidesaddle or astride. Finally, I decided that I might as well ride full saddle. Immediately, all other riders and horses behind me disappeared as I took control of the reins and rode full speed ahead, feeling an exhilaration I had not felt since horseback riding when I was a girl.

Step Two - Title

Step Three - Associate (Write down what you underlined and possible meanings. Guess!)

Step Four - Interpret (Weave what you've written above into a brief story.)

Step Five - Act (Write a possible action the dreamer might take.)

Interpretation - Second Dream

<u>Step One - Record</u>

I dreamed of walking in the <u>desert</u>. I felt <u>relief</u> to be away from home and I identified with the <u>nothingness</u> of my surroundings. Then a <u>man on horseback</u> followed by <u>two others</u> rode up and <u>kidnapped</u> me, sweeping me off my feet. I rode behind this first rider, sidesaddle, frightened. The <u>horses</u> changed appearance to something akin to stuffed stage horses with very hairy legs. I was faced with the <u>dilemma</u> of continuing sidesaddle or astride. Finally, I decided that I might as well ride full saddle. Immediately, all other riders and horses behind me disappeared as I took control of the reins and rode full speed ahead, feeling an <u>exhilaration</u> I had not felt since horseback riding when I was a girl.

<u>Step Two - Title</u>

"Taking the Reins"

<u>Step Three - Associate</u>

<u>desert</u> = my current arid existence

<u>relief</u> and <u>nothingness</u> = feelings of relief and nothingness

<u>horses</u> = powerful emotions

<u>three riders</u> = husband (the first rider) and two children (the two other riders)

<u>kidnapped</u> = marital dissatisfactions, forces carrying me off against my will

<u>dilemma</u> = to chose between riding passively in life or taking charge

<u>exhilaration</u> = a great feeling

Step Four - Interpret

Despite her effort and contentment in retreating into nothingness, her family situation has swept her off her feet and made off with her. Many of her domestic difficulties are due to staging (play-acting), although with serious problems in their foundations (hairy legs). She and her reined-in emotions are being carried away, but she always has the choice of being passive or active. The dream told her that, if she chooses to take the reins, to take control, her emotions will instantly become exhilarating as they were when she was a child riding horses.

Step Five - Act

She contemplated taking the reins. In time, she took them, to her great satisfaction.

+ + +

Final - Third Dream

Interpret a young man's dream in the space below or on a separate sheet of paper. Then compare it with the version on pp. 168-169.

Step One - Record (Underline key signifiers.)

> DREAM 087 - I wandered through my second-floor bedroom, my actual one. I was curious to see the ceiling covered by a mirror-like substance, which had partially shattered, covering the floor with sharp pieces and making walking difficult. The shattering revealed soggy insulation between the ceiling and the attic above. During the dream, I attributed the breakage of the mirror-like substance to the sogginess.

Step Two - Title

Step Three - Associate (Write down what you underlined and possible meanings. Guess!)

Step Four - Interpret (Weave what you've written above into a brief story.)

Step Five - Act (Write a possible action the dreamer might take.)

Interpretation - Dream Three

<u>Step One - Record</u>

>I wandered through my second-floor bedroom, the actual one in my <u>house</u>. I was curious to see the ceiling covered by a <u>mirror-like substance</u>, which had partially shattered, covering the floor with <u>sharp pieces</u> and making walking difficult. The shattering revealed <u>wet insulation</u> <u>between the ceiling and the attic</u> above. During the dream, I attributed the breakage of the mirror-like substance to the sogginess.

<u>Step Two - Title</u>

 "Soggy Protection"

<u>Step Three - Associate</u>

> <u>wet insulation</u> = inadequate house insulation with winter a month away; the wetness reminded the dreamer of a jog the previous morning in the rain
>
> <u>house</u> = the self
>
> <u>between the ceiling and the attic</u> = a wet ceiling-attic connection suggesting a throat vulnerability, the wetness was where the house's bedroom (upper body) joins its attic (head)
>
> (shattered) <u>mirror substance</u> = inability to look at self accurately
>
> <u>sharp pieces</u> (on bedroom floor) = preventing rest

Step Four - Interpret

(1) A recent decision to postpone reinforcing house insulation will cause problems this winter and in future ones.

(2) Yesterday's soaking in a cold drizzle will cause a break in health unless precautions are taken.

(3) I substitute passive curiosity for self-reflection and am not clearly seeing myself and the situation I'm in. As a consequence, I lack rest (bedroom), have to tread cautiously through life, and undertake efforts at self-improvement only half-heartedly.

The dream told me to (1) install home insulation, (2) bundle up outside and inside and instantly take other cold-preventative measures, and (3) begin daily self-reflection.

Step Five - Act

I did nothing in the short term. Because I didn't install insulation, I suffered winter cold and heating bills. By ignoring warnings of oncoming illness, days later I was bedridden with a severe sore throat. However, from my sick bed, I began self-reflection, including on the merits of acquiring an active, not passive, attitude toward life. On arising, I eased passage through that winter by at least plugging door and window drafts.

+ + +

Final - Dream Four

<u>Step One - Record</u> (Underline key signifiers.)

> DREAM 088 - I dreamed of a panorama of four beautiful, sunlit, rolling green hills, each with a milestone on top. They were seen from above as if through a floating television camera. The dream abruptly shifted to an evening rush-hour bus. It was totally dark outside. A woman was calling in via a two-way radio near the driver. She was lost. I wanted to assist and started up a conversation, asking many irrelevant questions such as her occupation and the foreign languages she spoke. I also offered some general advice, promising to check around and call her back. She was grateful, but contact was broken before I asked how to radio her again.

<u>Step Two - Title</u>

<u>Step Three - Associate</u> (Write down what you underlined and possible meanings. Guess!)

<u>Step Four - Interpret</u> (Weave what you've written above into a brief story.)

<u>Step Five - Act</u> (Write a possible action the dreamer might take.)

Interpretation - Dream Four

Step One - Record

I dreamed of a panorama of <u>four</u> beautiful, sunlit, rolling green <u>hills</u>, <u>each with a milestone</u> on top. They were seen from above as if through a floating television camera. The dream abruptly shifted to an evening rush-hour <u>bus</u>. It was <u>totally dark</u> outside. A woman was calling in via a two-way radio near the driver. She was lost. <u>I wanted to assist</u> and started up a conversation, asking many <u>irrelevant questions</u> such as her occupation and the foreign languages she spoke. I also offered some general advice, promising to check around and call her back. She was grateful, but contact was broken before I asked her how to radio her again.

StepTwoTitle

"More to Learn"

Step Three - Associate

<u>hills</u> = the route will have ups and downs but will be beautiful

<u>milestones</u> = four significant stages to go through in life

<u>bus</u> = on a fixed route, being driven by someone else, traveling with the crowd

<u>totally dark</u> = obscurity (night), unclearness

<u>two-way</u> radio = communication with the Beyond (e.g., the subconscious)

<u>I wanted to assist</u> = I'm helping another to meditate and like to assist others

<u>irrelevant</u> questions = a tendency toward wordiness in conversation

<u>Step Four - Interpret</u>

(1) I have four milestones ahead in life.

(2) I must first get off my fixed course (bus), out of the obscurity I travel in, and out from not being in the driver's seat. I seek to help and am well intentioned, but I need to ask relevant questions, avoid the irrelevant ones, and focus on what is most important (right in front of me) before I can assist with communications and, regarding two other interests, in meditation and the psychic (two-way radio).

(3) I also would best use more care in phrasing my questions.

<u>Step Five - Act</u>

I began to practice getting to the heart of matters, in conversations and elsewhere. I return to this dream periodically, counting the milestones as they occur. Time is precious, the miles to go numerous.

+ + +

"Two Moons" and Your Final Exam, Part II

Answer the questions below—we recommend very briefly. Use this page or a separate sheet of paper. Compare your answers with those at the end of Chapter Twenty-two.

1. What was the essential message of "Two Moons"?

2. What final advice do you have for the dreamer?

<u>Extra Credit</u>

3. In the next-to-last scene, the two moons did not quite merge. In the last scene, the two dogs and the dreamer did. Explain why.

22 | FINALE

To conclude Part Two: additional dream-related activities. pre-dream preparation, and answers to the "Two Moons" questions in Chapter 21.

Now What?

1. Attend a dream lecture, seminar, workshop, or class. See the Yellow Pages, newspaper ads, library bulletin boards, community college class schedules, and the Web.

2. Visit www.dreamlady.com and other dream-related Web sites. Ours has links to check out. Find out more by using an Internet search engine to look up "dreams," "analysis," "interpreting," and other dream-related terms.

3. Read. Reread *DreamLady.com,* the book, and absorb more. Buy a dream book, borrow one from a friend, or check one out from the public library, where you can also look up magazine articles and other dream references.

Pre-Sleep CheckList

Here's one way to check out of the world each night.

(1) Perform Preliminary Prep

Teeth brushed. Radio and TV off. Book reading and conversation ended. Pillow propped.

(2) Perform Dream Log Maintenance

Review one past dream, maybe two, in your log. Add new interpretations and other thoughts.

(3) Record a Dream to be Programmed (if any)

If you are into suggesting dreams, write in your log the dream suggestion for the evening and date it.

(4) Set Up Your Journal and Writing Instrument

Place your dream log and pen or pencil within easy reach and in the same location each night, ready for the next awakening's recording activity.

(5) Unprop Pillow and Lights Out

(6) Program a Dream (if you are going to)

Take a few slow, deep breaths. Relax. Think your suggestion three times with feeling.

(7) Fall Asleep

Sweet dreams!

"Two Moons" and the Conclusion

Dear Dreamer,

This is a dream about the integration of two feminine aspects.
One relates to the wise older woman within all women. The dream said that you should identify with this part of your being. Trust and listen to her. She's the part of you that is peaceful, all knowing, stoic, instinctive, and spiritual. Get to know her.
The other aspect is that of girl, daughter, mother, wife, lover, and temptress. This is the source of a woman's innocence, enthusiasm, passion, nurturing, sharing, and enchantment. Your dream suggested that this aspect is dominant and separate from the wise woman.
The two moons spectacularly symbolized these two separated parts. When the moons rose from maximum separation to almost touching, they suggested that you were close to integration and close to accepting and owning this integration or wholeness. Charles's presence reflects his involvement in this process. Their merging symbolizes the integration of Knowing and Emotions, and a higher vantage point from which to interact with the impermanence and permanence of close relationships on your roads of life.
Integration of these two feminine sides may not be easy. The dream indicated that they had almost merged and, in the dream, had you experiencing what happens when they touch. This was the happiness when you and your two female dogs united into an integrated whole—three essences in one inseparable pile rolling in the snow. What a great scene! This was when understanding of impermanence and permanence hit home. The dream says that good road companions are permanent (one is always around) and that it is the nature of things that particular ones are impermanent (their faces come and go). But the special ones are permanent—they always return in our memories, hearts, and dreams.
"Two Moons" tells you that there is a field beyond life's road, where

the essences of all good road companions permanently reside. Interestingly, in classical mythology, the souls of the good reside in the Elysian Fields, a place of peace.

Your winter moons illuminated the dark with a powerful glow, which was cold, silent, reflecting, passive, and stoic. In like fashion, permanent intuitive knowing and deep feeling illuminate impermanence. Your dream also gave its seal of approval to your relationship with Charles and to your inner journey to wholeness.

Leave lots of space in your journal for this one. Come back from time to time to decipher still more. New dreams will provide additional insights and tell of your progress.

Thanks for sharing a wonderful dream. We enjoyed it as much as you did. It has meaning for all of us. So, some thoughts to play with, contemplate, and sleep on.

Sweet dreams.
DreamLady and DreamKnight

+ + +

PART SIX

ADVANCED DREAM ANALYSIS

Interpretations by DreamLady

"Orion and the Swan"
"War in the Homeland"
"Negative Incantations"
"Tale of Two Beaus"
"The Book of the Shadows"
"The Daughter Who Repeatedly Falls Into Water"
"Where's High School Class?"
"Gunfight at Metro Credit"
"The Cattle Show"
"Airport Farewell"
"No Escape Through Hospital Walls"
"The Never-Ending Exam"

23 | ONE DOZEN DREAMS BY DREAMLADY

The full-length text of twelve dreams interpreted by DreamLady

Advanced Dream Analysis...

...is the level at which DreamLady Marilyn Peterson operates. Using dreams submitted to www.dreamlady.com with little or no personal information, she e-mails back interpretations, which are spontaneous, intuitive, helpful, and amazingly fast.

In the dreams below, you'll see points from the preceding chapters—principles, tips, and meanings—but no five-step approach. Marilyn's interpretations are free flowing—she's been doing them for forty years and was a natural from the start. Her approach, presented in these pages, on www.dreamlady.com, in her seminars, consultations, and interviews, is available to everyone. But no matter what approach you use or are developing, the purpose here is to encourage people to understand and benefit from their dreams.

So, a dozen pure DreamLady interpretations. Enjoy and learn.

DREAM 089 - "Orion and the Swan"

Dear DreamLady,

First, a little background. In 1999, I lost my beloved cocker spaniel Orion to cancer. I was grief-stricken and in 2000 I contacted a pet psychic to see if Orion would ever come back to me. She said that he would if my husband and I wanted that. I asked how I would know. She said he would come in a dream and tell me that he was born and to come pick him up. Well, we looked at several cocker pups and waited for the dream. Nothing happened. Finally, we settled on getting a golden retriever in December 2001, put the money down, and waited for him to be eight weeks old before getting him. The week we were supposed to get him we were told he got sick and was not expected to survive. We were shocked, and because we were prepared for a pup, we went to the animal shelter and picked up not one but two mixed breed pups and brought them home in January 2002. Now, two days ago (i.e., November 2002), I got this dream.

In a dream within this dream, Orion comes and tells me he is born and for us to come get him. When I dream that I wake up from this dream within a dream, I tell my husband, and we both wonder how we are going to get him when we already have these two dogs, who are difficult enough to manage. Finally, we decide that, because he asked, we will go and get him anyway. (I don't know how we find out where he is, but we get him home.) He is now a mixed color: part cocker spaniel with white, beige, and brown markings. Strangely, after he comes, we don't see our current two dogs around anymore. We take Orion on a walk and suddenly we come near a dense wooded area with huge tall banana trees, spaced so closely together that no sunlight can enter there. I am telling my husband, "Do you see that wood? If our dog ever goes in there, we are never going to be able to find him." Just as I speak, Orion runs away into the woods, and I think, "That is it! We have lost him." But he soon returns with a white swan in his mouth, and I think, "Oh no! He has killed that swan," but he gently lays it down at my feet and I realize he rushed into the woods to save the swan. I look forward to your interpretation. Thanks a million.

Dreamer

= = =

Dear Dreamer,

A dream within a dream—in other words, when you think you wake up but are still dreaming—is a very important dream. Your dream has a message for you and your husband. It is telling you that Orion is always with you, whether he comes back as another dog or whether he is there in spirit. You say in the dream that if he gets lost in the woods, you'll never find him, but Orion finds you. In fact, I think that Orion will lead both you and your husband to a new understanding of life after death. In the dream, Orion returns with a swan. In many religions, the swan is the symbol for the soul, and often, for the spirit. Orion has rescued that for you and brought it home to you. Now you know that love and devotion do not cease with death, but continue on in other dimensions that are available to you as well.

Keep watching your dreams, especially those where Orion shows up, and see what other lessons are available. With the two new dogs, your life seems fulfilling and, with Orion at your side in the spirit world, it sounds like you'll have a happy and rewarding life. Your story is very touching and meaningful to those who have lost someone or a pet who they dearly love.

DreamLady

+ + +

DREAM 090 - "War in the Homeland"

Dear DreamLady,

Last night I dreamt of me in a real-life situation of wartime!!! I witnessed the horror and the fear of the war together with my loved ones—all my friends and family! I saw the bombing of the houses. The destruction of my homeland! What does it mean?

                      Dreamer

= = =

Dear Dreamer,

I can understand how terrifying this dream must be for you. I can also assure you that it is not a prophetic dream. Usually dreams like this are presenting our own fears, especially in a time like this when the world is so troubled. It could also be symbolic of some of the things you are now facing with your family. Maybe it is not as peaceful as you would like. Are there occurrences of fighting, arguments, or family members flaring up and shouting at one another? Spend some time trying to identify what it could be describing within your family. Then watch your dreams. Your dreams will tell you more. Especially after you've studied a dream like this one, another dream will come along quickly that will give you more information.

Let me hear from you if this has been helpful.

                      DreamLady

+ + +

DREAM 091 - "Negative Incantations"

Dear DreamLady,

I have been having dreams with a recurrent theme—two just before I wake in the morning. They center around the idea of magic invocations draining the life force. Freaky! The first was with my mother and sister, who were trying to invoke an animal spirit. They had found the spell and workings and decided to do them while I tried to dissuade them. They created a hyena man who had huge gaping black holes where his eyes should be. The next morning, I dreamt that I was in my garden at home and my mum was going to sacrifice me. She wanted my life force and essence so that she could become young again, but I managed to win the fight and she collapsed on me. I was scared that she was dying. Then I woke up. Neither dream had a conclusion—I seemed to wake myself up mid dream. It's strange and worries me.

Dreamer

= = =

Dear Dreamer,

Your dream is telling you about your relationship with your mother and sister. It is saying that you feel they are cooking up something together that you don't approve of. The hyena man could be a man who just laughs at them, but you also know he can't see and is blind to what is happening. The second dream again tells you that you fear that your mother is trying to use your energies, motivations, and desires to get what she wants rather than what you want. Although you win this time, you are afraid that it is dangerous for her or that she might have a collapse of some kind. The dream picture is taking place in your garden, which could mean that it is something that has happened previously. The back of the house often symbolizes the past. Because it's in a garden, where things grow naturally, it could be showing you that, in some ways, this is a natural thing that happens when a child grows up and the mother grows older. Perhaps she is wishing that she could have some of the things that you either have now or can expect as your life unfolds.

Try to identify, if you can, what the earlier dream might be referencing. Perhaps this is an instance in which your mother and your sister agree. Then think about other times, such as your mother wanting to share some of your experiences or live vicariously through them. Then watch your dreams to learn more about the situation with your mother and sister. Your dreams will help you build a happy, prosperous, and fulfilled life. Let me know if my comments have been helpful and worthwhile.

DreamLady

+ + +

DREAM 092 - "Tale of Two Beaus"

Dear DreamLady,
   (Background) I am a virgin. I never had a condom in my coat and never saw the dream house I was in before. I have never had a sexual dream before.
   My boyfriend and I are on the couch making out with each other in the living room. He is wearing his favorite red sweatshirt, which I love. I love the way that he kisses, so I tell him so. Soon, things start to get really hot, and some clothes to come off. I tell my boyfriend that I will go get a condom. I go to my jacket and pull out a condom. When I start to turn around, I see my best friend from high school, Evan. He is the guy whom I always liked in high school, but who would never give me a chance. I asked what Evan was doing there and where my boyfriend was. He asked what I was talking about. I told him that I was going out with Carl and that Evan shouldn't be there. I said that I finally found a guy that I really like and that I was not going to break up with Carl for him again. Evan started to get mad, so I tried to run away. I got to the kitchen, but he grabbed my arm and whipped me around. Then I woke up. My left arm hurt.
Dreamer

===

Dear Dreamer,
   Your dream is telling you of your relationship with your current boyfriend. But even more important, it is telling you about how your feelings about sex and love are changing. Whereas before, it was the way it was, now, your dream is showing that you and your boyfriend are moving toward a closeness that is deeper than you've had with other guys. Even the guy you were scoping out in the past is not the type of person that you want to share yourself with. You understand that real intimacy, regardless of whether it is physical or emotional, requires something more. The house represents a new state of mind, a state of consciousness that is housing these new feelings. The condom in the

coat is saying that you are beginning to realize that things may go further than they have gone in the past and that you want to be prepared. That way, you don't risk having unsafe sex, if physical intimacy is part of the future, whether near or far in the future. Back in the dream, you say that you hide in the kitchen. We all know that frustrations often result in sublimation. Be careful you don't overeat as a way to either placate your desires or to shut down your body with fullness. The fact that he grabs your arm in the dream and it is sore when you wake up is the dream's way of reminding us that the issue being pictured is very real. Don't fool yourself that this is just fantasy. It is a good dream and I feel that you are making wonderful strides in growth and understanding. Keep watching your dreams and learn more. Your dreams will help you build a happy, prosperous, and fulfilled life.

DreamLady

+ + +

DREAM 093 - "The Book of the Shadows"

Dear DreamLady,

I was in a forest. It was almost dusk. I am uneasy, but not afraid. I am alone. I see a book bound in leather. It is very large and old. It is lying amongst damp autumn leaves and almost blends in with the ground completely. I move toward it and read the title scripted across the front, "The Book of the Shadows." I suddenly become very frightened, too scared to open it. At that moment, I become aware of a presence, although I can't see anyone. I become very scared and start to run.

Dreamer

= = =

Dear Dreamer,

Your dream is telling you that recently you realized there were other parts to yourself that were different than the you that you are familiar with. This part of yourself, up until now, has been unknown to you. You might have thought, "That somehow doesn't seem like me," or simply, "I don't know why I said that," or, "Why I did I do that?," or, "I've never felt that way before." These are signals that you are about to become aware of the shadow part of yourself. Of course, this can be scary because it will change our self-image. However, to become a complete person, what the psychologists call individuation, it is necessary for us to become not only aware of, but also accepting of, our shadows. It's called integration. So when people in your dreams are the same sex as you are, they are called the shadow.

Well, it seems you have cut right to the chase and have come upon the whole story (the book). The dream showed you in a forest, which is a symbol for the natural growth process. The leaves are a symbol for things in the past. You are being shown that the book is important looking and so important for you at this time. The feeling that there was another presence is saying that your shadow is really a presence in your life now. This is an excellent time to get to know more about how you really feel about things (not what you've been taught to feel or what is right to feel). Not only feelings, but actions and lifestyles, etc. You might want to check at your library to read more about what Carl Jung, the noted Swiss psychologist, has written about the shadow. One book I can recommend is <u>The Meaning in Dreams and Dreaming</u> by Maria Mahoney, a Jungian analyst. Also, I believe Esther Harding's book, <u>Way of All Women</u>, does a good job of shedding some light on the shadow. Keep watching your dreams and learn more. Your dreams will help you build a happy, prosperous, and fulfilled life.

  Hope this helps.

DreamLady

+ + +

DREAM 094 - "The Daughter Who Repeatedy Falls Into Water"

Dear DreamLady,

Thank you for helping me out here. I've had a recurring dream for the last seven-and-a-half years. Please help! My dream is about my youngest daughter. It seems like each time we plan to go to the local zoo, the evening before, I dream that she is in the hippo exhibit and falls into the water. By the time I go to help, I wake up. In another dream we were walking near a small bayou on a busy road. When we walked by, she fell through the bridge gates and again, by the time I went to help her, I woke up.

(Background) I get crazy whenever we are near water and I avoid taking my kids swimming every summer.

Dreamer

= = =

Dear Dreamer,

I can certainly understand your feelings. How terrifying! However, I can honestly say that I don't see anything in the dream that would indicate that these dreams are precognitive or that they even predict that the child is in danger around water. When my children were young, I had three little girls, and I was afraid that, if they fell in the pool, I couldn't save all of them. When they were four, I made sure each had swimming lessons. In fact, they became swim champions. You might want to make sure that your children know how to swim. They learn very easily when they're young, and I can attest that it brings incredible peace of mind.

Your dream is telling you about your relationship with your daughter. It shows that you have fears about her growing up. Water in a dream is a symbol for life and emotion. You might want to ask yourself if you are reluctant for her to grow up in any way. Does it relate to a fear that she won't be prepared for life and might be overwhelmed by it? Falling through the gate, as you described from the bayou dream, could be a picture for falling through the cracks, which is one of the things that happen to children who are the youngest in the family. You might want to look at the hippo exhibit. It could relate to a fear about her size, or maybe a big mouth (as in telling things that shouldn't be told) or some other tendency that she is currently exhibiting.

Water in a dream is also the symbol for mother and for time. Because this has been going on for some time, you might want to look at your own concept of yourself as a mother. Also, see if there could be something about the time when she'll be old enough to leave home.

I hope this helps. Keep watching your dreams. Now that you've looked at the earlier dreams in this light, see if your dreams change. Your dreams will help you build a happy, fulfilled, and safe life for you and your children.

Please let me know if my comments have been helpful.

DreamLady

+ + +

DREAM 095 - "Where's High School Class?"

Dear DreamLady,

I have always been fascinated by dreams and was hoping that you might analyze one dream that I consider to be recurring. I haven't had this dream for a while but I used to have it quite regularly and just thought it would be interesting to hear your thoughts on it. I dream that I am back in high school and I cannot find my next class or sometimes I can't find my locker. Either way, I am lost and wandering around the school continuously. Just wondering if you might shed some light on this.

Dreamer

= = =

Dear Dreamer,

Your recurring dream about going back to high school and being unable to find your next class or your locker is a very common dream that many, many people have.

The dream is showing you that, whereas earlier in your life you had more of an understanding of what you were learning and why, today you find that identifying the lessons and working at finding ways to learn from your experiences is much more difficult.

In a way, it is much better, or at least easier, for things to be spelled out clearly. You know what is expected, what you need to do in order to be acceptable, etc. But as you mature, you realize that the lessons life has in store for us are not so clear cut. You feel lost because you don't know what's next.

Because you haven't had this dream for a while, perhaps you are getting more in tune with the lessons you're currently dealing with. Or maybe you are handling them better.

Keep watching your dreams and learn more. Your dreams will help you build a happy, prosperous, and fulfilled life. Please let me know if you start having new types of dreams that relate to life's lessons.

I hope this helps.

DreamLady

+ + +

DREAM 096 - "Gunfight at Metro Credit"

Dear DreamLady,

My dream was actually a movie trailer, and I was a star in the movie. It started with me and two of my friends in an old, big convertible. I was riding in the front seat. My friends, Nate and Roger, were in the back seat, and Eminem, the rap artist, was driving. We pulled up in front of an office building much like the one in the movie, "The Matrix." We proceeded inside and had a huge gunfight with a security team and a SWAT team, once again much like in "The Matrix." Once Eminem, my friends, and I killed all of the security guards and the SWAT team members, my sister came in and gave a really corny punch line/catch phrase. It was something like, "Now your balance is overdue!" It makes sense because the camera scans up to the name of the business's office building, which was something like "Metro Credit Union," or something like that. Then the announcer said, "Coming to a credit company near you." Then I woke up and wrote down some notes.

Dreamer

= = =

Dear Dreamer,

Your dream is telling you about what is happening in your life, where you are the star. The convertible is a symbol of your drives and motivations. Your friends are taking the back seat in recent activities. You're up front with the driver. Eminem, the rap artist, is driving, so if you want to know what's driving you and your friends to do what you're doing, you need to identify Eminem's main message in his rap. Or if you were telling someone who Eminem is, what would you say?

The entire reference to "The Matrix," again, is something you'll have to label. Is it a parallel universe, or what? But, whatever it is, it brings you face to face with things like security, the "heavy duty protectors," and the special weapon and tactical team. When this happens, some-

thing related to you. Something more intuitive, more feeling rather than thinking, and more attached to home (your sister) tells you that you are getting too out of balance with this new lifestyle you're building for yourself. Even the business office, which could relate to the college administration, or something related to your grades (or credits), is saying that it is coming close to you and bearing down. The fact that you wake up then, when you realize what you're risking, has the dream bringing to your conscious mind that you are facing a conflict—that is, whether to continue in the way you've been going and jeopardize you college career or whether you're going to try to live a more balanced life so you can stay in school and graduate. The dream is saying that it means business, and if I were you, I would carefully consider the issues.

I hope this helps.

DreamLady

+ + +

DREAM 097 - "The Cattle Show"

Dear DreamLady,

I was with my family. We were at a cattle show looking at cattle. I kept saying to my mom, "No, Mom, no," and she said, "It's going to be all right."

(Background) Some things you should know. I grew up on a farm. I just started college. I am nineteen years old and close with my mom.

Dreamer

= = =

Dear Dreamer,

Your dream is telling you that you are now facing a different situation than when you were living at home. The cattle show is the vast array of choices you are now facing at school.

It could also be a symbol for going along with the rest of the students like cattle move along with the herd.

Some of this is neither what you had expected nor what you wanted. But your mother is telling you that it will be okay. Although it seems overwhelming now, with all the activities, choices, types of people you're meeting, their backgrounds, etc., she is saying that you will be able to keep your own individuality and make choices that will help you build a happy, successful, and fulfilling life at school and in the future. For now, keep the communications open with your mother. She can help you and be very supportive for you as you find your way through all of the things you're facing. It is a good dream. Your feelings are normal and reflect the way everybody feels when they first go away to school. You're fortunate that you have strong family ties that will be supportive as you make your way.

Keep watching your dreams. They will help you build a good life. Hope this helps.

DreamLady

+ + +

DREAM 098 - "Airport Farewell"

Dear DreamLady,

I am with Tom Cruise, driving out to the airport in a convertible. However, I leave him in the parking lot while I go into the airport. There I find myself following Nicolas Cage. I keep behind him because I don't want him to see me. He is departing. As he is ready to go through the passageway to the plane, suddenly, he turns and sees me. I see that there's a tear in his eye.

Dreamer

===

Dear Dreamer,

Your dream is showing you that you are appreciated, understood, and adored by at least two people who have been or are now in your life. However, a choice is required at this time. Should you choose a relationship in which you can "cruise" through life, happy and carefree? Or should you choose to go along with the other, who is a "cage." Regardless of how loving, a velvet cage or silk cage is still a cage. Both restrict as much as a cage with steel bars.

You wake at this point because you haven't yet made the choice and there is still unresolved conflict about what to do.

Try to identify the situation that you're facing and that requires this choice and see if the stars in this dream shed some light or even amplify some of the issues involved.

I hope this helps.

DreamLady

+ + +

DREAM 099 - "No Escape Through Hospital Walls"

Dear DreamLady,
 Today I had lunch with a dear older friend, who's eighty years old. She told me about a vivid dream she had several times when she was in the hospital for an inflammation in her back that gave her lots of pain. She dreamed she was in a dark room and wanted to get out. There were striations on the walls. She wanted to get through the wall, but she couldn't. She did make dents in the wall but she couldn't get through it. What did that mean???

Friend of Dreamer

= = =

Dear Dreamer,
 Your dream is telling you about your valiant efforts to get through the confinement (walls) of the situation that you've been in (hospital stay). The darkness means that you're not exactly aware of the cause of the pain, but nevertheless, you are determined to get through it. You're able to make some progress periodically, but so far have been unsuccessful in getting out of the situation entirely. Not that you're trying to get out of the hospital per se, but that you are trying to get through the pain by breaking down the walls that are causing it. The dream is showing you that there are striations on the walls, which may give you a clue as to what the problem is all about.
 Health dreams can often visually portray the problem (for example, a wall of muscles). If so, the marks on the wall may be your muscle striations. I looked it up and learned that the voluntary muscles in the body have dark and light bands that clothe the vertebrate skeleton. That is, masses of fibers with transversely striated bands are directly connected with the bones that we control. Healthy muscles connected to the vertebrae are flexible and open. Inflammation causes swelling and pain. It could be that the room is depicting the space within you where the striated bands of muscles are like a wall of pain, rigid and inflexible (like a wall), that has you and your vertebrae blocked in. To stop the pain, this wall must be broken down.

Your dream shows that you were making dents in it through the therapy you received in the hospital, but require more rest, relaxation, and other therapies over time to relax the rigid muscular walls that enclose the vertebrae. This would be a good dream to tell your doctor.
 I hope this is helpful.

DreamLady

+ + +

DREAM 100 - "The Never-Ending Exam"

Dear DreamLady,
   (Background). I graduated many years ago.
   I took a final exam of a university class. The professor was very lax. All other students had finished, but remained in the classroom noisily complaining about the toughness and fairness of the exam. I tuned out the noise and diligently continued, but I was stuck on an unfamiliar section. I reread it several times, but kept losing my place in the exam booklet. I looked elsewhere in the booklet for clues, without success. I didn't know what the exam was on or even what the class was about. I looked at the wall clock frequently—1:04 p.m., 1:07 p.m., almost the end of the test hour. Then, 1:10 p.m., and time was up. Here I was, the last person still taking the test, and the professor said nothing. So I kept on and on pondering the unfamiliar section. Was it an assignment that I had not read?

Dreamer

= = =

Dear Dreamer,

Anxiety about exams is one of the more common dreams and may relate to feelings of not being prepared, inadequacy, and not measuring up, whether or not you have an actual test the next day. Your dream is telling you to examine your standards. It sounds like your pursuit of excellence has you seeking to answer and complete all things, great and small, rather than first questioning the allotted time and the question itself.

This is a dream about your approach to answering the tasks in front of you. It is telling you that, first, it is a question of time. The other students knew when to stop and so did you. You do not need an authority (the professor) or anyone else to tell you, "Stop!" It's over when it's over. In this case, 1:10 p.m. was the precise moment to bring the exam to closure and go on to other things, rather than to go on and on past the given time.

Second, the dream is telling you it's a question of answering the question and no more.

A helpful technique for dreams that have unsatisfying endings or non-endings is to rewrite them. For example, if it were my dream, I'd respond to the troublesome question by writing, "I don't know," and hand in the exam at 1:10 p.m. The dream professor immediately arouses from his passive state, reads it, smiles, and says, "You pass!" The impossible trick question had tested for honest answers, not fudged ones, and for submission on time without being asked.

Hope this helps.

DreamLady

+ + +

INDEX

A

act 3, 6, (What to do With a Dream?) 36, 49-51, 122-123, 155, 156
analyze dreams - see interpret dreams
anxiety dreams (including nightmares) 93-94, 95-103, 124, 133-134, 153-154, 185-186, 187-188, 189-190,191-192, 198-199,
associate 3, 4-5, 45-46, 131-132, 133-134, 138-139

B

birth - see transition

C

checklists - see lists
children's dreams 157-158, 191-192
components 57, 63-64
cover photo - see www.allthesky.com

D

dead, the - see transition
death - see transition
dream analysis - see interpret
dreams, components of - see list
dreams, nature of xi, 35-38, 15, see purpose
DreamLady (bio) xi-xiii, 183
dying - see transition

E

emotions - see mood

F

fragments, dreams - see segments
feelings - see mood
Fill-in-the-Gaps Checklist - see list

H

historical dreams 104-107

I

integration 33, 61, 80, 103, 135, 144, 158, 189
interpret dreams (5 Steps) 3-11, (basic) 12-19, (a chapter of) 20-34, (5 Steps revisited) 39-52, (checklist) 41-43, (advanced) 127-144, 153-154, (final exam) 160-173
interpretations, complete by DreamLady 99-101, 181-201
interpretations, instant - see puns
interpretations, literal 5, 12, 38, 47, 52, 71, 72, 79, 85, 87, 108, 109, 112, 133-134, 139, 140
interpretations, symbolic 4, 6, 12, 33, 36, 38, 47, 54, 71, 73, 103, 109, 112, 134, 135, 155, 156, 176, 183, 184, 185, 186, 189, 190, 192, 194, 196

L

levels, dream 48, 75, 85, 105, 137-138, 145
life forms 12, (Who?) 41, 64, 75-80
link - see associate
list - components of dreams 57, 63-64
list - (checklist) Fill-In-The-Gaps 41-43
list - What Are Dreams? 35-36
list - What a Dream Can Do For You 36-37
list - What To Do With a Dream 36
list - Now What? 174
list - Pre-Sleep Checklist 175

list - Special Dreams 93-94
list - techniques, more advanced (on one page) 117
literal - see interpretations
location - see setting

M

maintenance 137-138, 145-148, 175
mood 7, 10, 17, 19, (5 Steps Expanded) 39-52, 54, 57, 70, 72, 78, 81-83, 86, 102-103, 121, 123, 127, 129-130, 132, 134, 160

N

nature of dreams - see dreams, nature
nightmare - see anxiety
Now What? - see list

O

odds and ends - see potpourri

P

plot 4, 40, 41, 45, 53, 57, 63-64, 69-74, 81, 93, 126, 127, 195
potpourri (colors, directions, other odds and ends) 84-91
Pre-Sleep Checklist - see list
program a dream 119-120, 142, 156
props 42, 84-86
psychic dreams 113-115, 159
pun, dream 13, 42, 47, 85, 141, 128, 160
purpose of a dream i, xi, 38, 181, see dreams, nature of

Q

questions 4, 5, 45, 48, 52, 75, 99, 100, 103, 131-132, 133, 138, 139-141, 151-159

R

record 3, 4, 40-44, 126, 148
recurring 36, 48, 52, 53-55, 59, 110, 122, 127, 128-129, 138, 141, 145, 146, 152, 185, 193
repeats - see recurring
remembering dreams 4, 17, 40, 41, 42, 43, 44, 79, 117, 119-126, 153, 154

S

segments, dream 14-15, 41, 44
setting 40, 42, 45, 53, 57, 62-68, 81, 93, 124, 129, 145, 146
signifier 12, 13, 53, 59, 63, 65, 76, 78, 80, 105, 109, 110, 112, 127, 128, 131, 133, 135, 136, 138, 139, 145, 154, 155, 156, 158, 160
signifier, key 13, 19, 20, 33, 57, 59, 84, 86, 89, 127, 128, 130, 131, 135-136, 138-141, 159, 160, 161
Sonandres (bio) xii, xiii
special dreams - see list
Steps, all (on one page) 3, (basic) 3-11, (expanded) 39-52
Step Five - see act
Step Four - see interpret
Step One - see record
Step Three - see associate
Step Two - see title
suggest a dream - see program
symbolic - see interpretation

T

theme 5, 8, 11, 45, 48, 53, 54, 55, 59-61, 62, 63, 82, 84, 86, 89, 93, 122, 127, 131, 143, 185
time 35, 42, (when) 43, 53, 57, 63-64, 65, 89, 106, 111, 112, 113, 130, 134, 135, 192, 198, 200-201
title a dream 3, 4, 5, 11, 20, 44, 47, 127, 128, 146, 148, 189
transition dreams (birth, death, dying, dead) 106, 108-112, 140

W

What a Dream Can Do For You - see list
What Are Dreams? - see list
What To Do With a Dream - see list
what - see props, potpourri
when - see time
where - see setting
who - see life forms
www.dreamlady.com i, iv, xi, xii, xiii, 99, 123, 141, 174, 181
www.allthesky.com (cover photo by Till Credner) iv, xiii